In Love a

Boundaries: that was the word I wanted—boundaries. Mr McIndoe dissolved them all, that was the problem, and so some women were coerced into things they didn't want to do. But it was probably what saved those young men's lives, made them want to live.

Gladys, a nurse

Having your face mashed up and burned does make you work out what's important. We were all in the same sort of shit, we all looked monstrous. We were all terrified of the future, being rejected by women, unable to work, treated as outcasts, packed off somewhere to be hidden away so we wouldn't frighten the children.

Roger*, a Guinea Pig

You got very close to them because you thought you might be dead tomorrow. You saw them every day and you did things for them that no one had done before, things they used to be able to do for themselves. You wanted to make them happy and do something for the war and you felt proud when you did. So you fitted in even if it went against what you thought was right.

Nancy*, a nurse

Some of the people interviewed for this book preferred not to be named. I have identified them with a first name only and indicated this with an asterisk. Liz Byrski, 2015

In Love and War
nursing heroes

Liz Byrski

Liz Byrski is the author of a number of non-fiction books including *Remember Me* and *Getting On: Some Thoughts on Women and Ageing,* as well as eight novels including *Gang of Four* and *Family Secrets*. She has worked as a freelance journalist, a broadcaster with ABC Radio and an advisor to a minister in the Western Australian Government. Liz has a PhD from Curtin University where she lectures in writing. Visit the author at **lizbyrski.com**.

For the women who nursed, loved, married
and danced with the Guinea Pigs

CONTENTS

1. MEMORIES

East Grinstead, Sussex

It's 1950, I'm six years old and I'm praying for peace. It began when Sister Walbert told the class that although The War ended years ago we must all pray very hard that there will never be another one. I don't know anything about The War. If people mention it, my parents glance anxiously in my direction, shake their heads and change the subject. But I know that my prayers aren't working, because there are men here from The War, men with terrible faces. They get on the bus in the town and get off at the hospital, and I'm sure they have a camp in Blackwell Hollow, a street bordered by steep walls of mossy rock and densely overhung with trees that keep it in a perpetual state of damp and mysterious darkness. One day, when Mum and I are waiting for the bus, the men will jump out from behind those rock walls and grab us. I screw up my face and ask God not to make another war. Most of all, I ask Him to take the men away or, as a last resort, to make Sister Walbert and my dad report them to the police. I ask God this every day but He continues to ignore me. Some days, in despair at my lack of success with silent prayer, I go out into the field at the back of our house and shout very loudly at Him, in the hope that He might hear.

After school on Wednesdays my mother takes me to Miss Perkins's dancing class. In white satin tunics we practise our pliés and arabesques while Miss Perkins—dark wavy hair, perfect Cupid's bow shaped with crimson lipstick—taps time with her stick. She wears high-heeled red shoes with ankle straps and red satin bows. I have seen Moira Shearer dance to her death on the railway lines in *The Red Shoes* and I fear an equally terrible end for Miss Perkins who, according to Mum, has already been forced to abandon her career as dancer due to a debilitating bone condition. After the dancing class Mum takes me out for tea and chocolate éclairs in Clarendon House Café, where no one speaks above a whisper and the waitresses are dressed in faded black with starched aprons and stiff white caps like little tiaras. We sit at a table by the diamond-pane, leadlight window. The air is heavy with the scent of tea-leaves, Coty face powder and 4711 Cologne. I love the hushed, elderly air of Clarendon House, the feathers and artificial flowers nodding on the customers' hats, the promise of shared secrets in their whisperings.

'You did very well today,' Mum says, 'especially with your arms. Last week you were like a windmill, but today you were quite graceful.'

My mother, herself a former teacher of dancing, has very high standards. I am in heaven: praise and chocolate éclairs. This is my favourite time of the week—until it's time to catch the bus home.

The men with the terrible faces are sitting on the wall by the bus stop with their livid crimson and purple skin, bulbous lips, missing ears, shapeless noses, and hands without fingers. They are living, breathing manifestations of the men who lurk on the stairs outside my bedroom door, who hide under my bed, who fill my nightmares. They are war heroes. I don't know what a hero is but I know they have brought The War here to East Grinstead. I am appalled that they are allowed to wander the streets, catch the buses and chat to Mum at the bus stop.

'No, silly!' my mother laughs, when I tell her she should get Dad to report them to the police. 'They're heroes from World War II, and that's all over now.'

I don't believe her. The men step aside to let us get on the bus first. They talk loudly and laugh a lot. One wears a leather flying jacket with a furry collar, another a cream ribbed cricket sweater, one has a silvery blue RAF greatcoat slung over his shoulder.

'Don't stare,' Mum whispers as the men get off the bus at the hospital. 'It's rude. You wouldn't like people to stare at you, would you?'

I'm not sure whether or not I would mind being stared at, but I both do and don't want to look at these men. I'm terrified of their faces but my eyes are drawn to them like pins to a magnet. One has a huge misshapen lump instead of a nose, another has a hole where one of his eyes should be and he carries a white stick. They stroll away from the bus stop into the hospital grounds and as the bus moves off, one turns back, his attempted smile a distorted gash of a grin in his crimson face; it's a grin that will haunt my dreams. He raises his bandaged hand to wave to me. I squeeze my eyes shut and yell silently to God to save me from the heroes. But God still isn't listening, not then and not later, because for years, the men with the terrible faces are still in town. Just when I think it's safe I suddenly find one standing alongside me, spot a couple on the steps of The Rose and Crown or talking to the man who slices the bacon in Sainsbury's.

East Grinstead, Sussex

It's late May 2007. I'm sixty-three. Because Clarendon House has been converted into offices I am sitting in the café section of The Bookshop from where I can see the High Street, the war memorial, the bus stop where we caught the 434 bus home from dancing class, and the wall where the men with the terrible faces sat waiting for the chance to kidnap Mum and me, or possibly just to get the bus back to the Queen Victoria Hospital where they were being treated for their chronic wartime burns. There are no war heroes here today, although there very easily could be, because the men of the RAF Fighter and Bomber Commands, of whom I was so scared as a child, have a long and affectionate relationship with this town. It was here that the casualties of the war in the air—their faces burned beyond recognition, their hands fingerless and unusable, their self-esteem in tatters—were reconstructed and rehabilitated by the pioneering plastic surgeon Sir Archibald McIndoe. They were his surgical 'guinea pigs' and with him they formed a club with the most exclusive membership in the world. To qualify for membership of the Guinea Pig Club a man had to be 'mashed, fried or boiled' by the war in the air, and to have been treated at East Grinstead.

By the end of World War II the club had 649 members. Each year they have returned in large numbers for their annual reunion. Today age, infirmity and distance are taking their toll and the club is winding down. The ninety-seven remaining members are spread across the world: nine in Australia, others in Canada, New Zealand and various European countries. Of the remaining fifty-seven in Britain, a handful live in or around East Grinstead, but some of those further afield are no longer able to make the trip back here. In October this year, 2007, the remaining few will gather to celebrate their sixty-fifth and final reunion, but the club, which has sustained them through the war and postwar years, will continue to provide support for them and for the fifty-six Guinea Pig widows with whom it has remained in touch.

From my window seat in the café section of The Bookshop, which is housed in one of a long run of timber-framed Tudor buildings in the High Street, this could be any small Sussex town. There are several points of historical note: a Jacobean almshouse, a sixteenth-century sandstone church, a significant National Trust property dating back to the Arts and Crafts movement, and the close proximity of Ashdown Forest, home of Winnie the Pooh and Christopher Robin. And early in the evening of 23rd July 1913, ten members of the East Grinstead Women's Suffrage Society set out to march along this street under their silk banner. It was just six weeks after suffragette Emily Wilding Davison had died after throwing herself under King George V's horse at the Derby. The women had just turned into the High Street when they encountered an angry mob of fifteen hundred anti-suffragists who began hurling ripe tomatoes, eggs and pieces of turf at them.[1]

In my childhood this bookshop was a stationer's shop and its windows overlooked the graves of three sixteenth-century

Protestant martyrs, the headstones set into the pavement. But a few years ago these were relocated to the churchyard to make space for the pavement tables of another café where once there was a bank. Even martyrs, it seems, must yield to commercial interests.

East Grinstead has some interesting religious connections. In addition to its Anglican and Catholic churches, and Opus Dei, the town is also home to other sects including the Rosicrucian Order, and the Mormons. In 1994, Channel 4 focused one of its *Witness* programs on the town, which, it suggested, was becoming the 'religious capital' of England. As well as featuring all of the above, the program also included The Pagan Federation, water diviners and, strangely out of context, the Guinea Pig Club.

Saint Hill, a magnificent manor house reputed to be the finest eighteenth-century sandstone building in Sussex, has had a series of distinguished owners in its time but best remembered is the writer and founder of Scientology, the late L. Ron Hubbard, who bought it from the Maharaja of Jaipur in 1959. Today it is the international headquarters of the Church of Scientology, which owns many other local properties. However, a significant period in its history was the wartime tenancy of Elaine and Neville Blond, friends of Archibald McIndoe, who opened up much of the house as a convalescent home for his patients.

But East Grinstead's greatest claim to fame is its relationship with those wartime heroes. Here, flyers with the worst imaginable burns underwent radical new procedures involving anything from three to more than fifty operations for which they returned regularly during the war and for more than a decade after it ended. The QVH—which began life as the East Grinstead Cottage Hospital in 1863—is the birthplace of some of the most significant developments in modern plastic surgery; it is Britain's leading centre for skin and wound repair, plus reconstructive and head and neck surgery. Alongside it, the associated but independent Blond McIndoe Research Foundation has been at the forefront of wound repair research for almost five decades. Archibald

McIndoe was not content with just physical reconstruction and repair. He was determined to restore the self-esteem of these wounded young men and to create a sense of the future in which others would see past their injuries to the men themselves. In a therapeutic experiment, extraordinary for its time, he involved the whole town in contributing to his patients' rehabilitation. He called on local residents to accept his patients, not to stare at or shy away from their disfigurement, but to look them in the eye, invite them into their homes and drink with them in the pubs. He made East Grinstead a safe haven for his Guinea Pigs and, in doing so, made life liveable again.

I sit here sipping coffee where my mother used to buy her Basildon Bond notepaper and my school exercise books. I am trying to reach back into the past and work out where to begin. I want to dig beneath this heroic myth—the stories of heroism, stoicism and dazzling surgical reconstruction. I want to know what it meant to be a dashing young flyer one day, and the next a potential social outcast with a face burned beyond recognition and mere stumps for hands, and what that means now, to men in their eighties and nineties. I want to know more about McIndoe the man: not just his surgical skill but his motivation, and how he involved a whole town in the process of rebuilding shattered lives. And I want to know about the nurses who must surely have their own stories. Some would have been excited by the prospect of working in the new discipline of plastic surgery. Some may have had husbands or lovers at the front, and some would have been young, in their late teens or early twenties, recruited into the war effort and thrust, with inadequate training, into a groundbreaking medical environment in which the usual social and professional boundaries had been dismantled. History has washed over the stories of these women, in the service of memorialising the heroes. The hidden corners of women's history always fascinate me and as a novelist I write the hidden stories of older women's lives. Now I want to know what nursing those men meant to the women who were at the front line of McIndoe's treatment. Over the years The Guinea

Pigs have told aspects of their stories in a very particular way that memorialises and concretises collective memory. But what about the untold stories—the half forgotten memories, the tales that might not fit?

This place, these men and their faces, have haunted me since childhood. Even now they are still a part of my dreams of impending disaster that include ceilings and walls which threaten to crush or suffocate me under piles of rubble. Knowing, for decades, that the Guinea Pigs are heroes who will do me no harm has not dispelled this haunting of my subconscious nor the chilling physical fear that the images create.

Late one summer evening, long after I should have been asleep, I hear my father's voice outside and creep to the open bedroom window. Through the dusk I can see the shapes of two dark-suited figures crossing the garden. Clutching my teddy I tiptoe to the top of the stairs from where I can see straight down to the front door. If my father sees me there he will come up and kiss me goodnight. I hold my breath for the sound of his key in the door. Dad comes in first. The visitor follows, looks up and sees me.

'You must be Elizabeth,' he says. His face is a mass of purple scars, stretched and shiny skin, his lips are bulbous; his eyes—one angled slightly lower than the other—seem to travel in different directions under the scarred and browless forehead. 'Your Dad's been telling me about you.' He puts a fingerless hand on the banister, his foot on the bottom step. 'Are you coming down?'

I have prayed—asked God to send the men away—but He has ignored me and, overwhelmed with terror, I step forward onto air.

When I come to later, in the emergency ward at the hospital, my parents are staring anxiously down into my face.

'You fainted, silly thing,' my mother said. 'You fell right down the stairs, and you've got a big cut where your head hit the door.'

The scar remains, tiny now, a reminder of what my reaction might have meant to the man whose face had terrified me. If there was a sin greater than staring at a disfigured face then surely it was fainting at the sight of one. Might I find that man? Might I see his face among the photographs, talk to him, and tell him how often I have thought of him and felt ashamed?

I crane my neck and look down towards the war memorial and see my mother as she was then: thirty-nine years old, tall and striking in a blue suit with square shoulders and a straight skirt, a rakish little hat anchored at an angle with a sequined pin. The child holding her hand is mousey, her hair cut square and pulled back from her face with a Kirby grip and a red and white check ribbon. She clings to her mother's hand, shifting to shelter behind her as the men with the terrible faces stroll up to the bus stop. One of them stops and looks at her, he bends forward, speaks and reaches out a mangled hand, but the child backs away, pressing her face into her mother's skirt.

2. BEGINNINGS

In the three weeks since I arrived, it's been raining most of the time. Parts of Yorkshire and the Midlands are flooded, and in Gloucestershire and Herefordshire, householders and shopkeepers have stopped equivocating about stocking up on supplies and are now preparing for the worst. Today is the first day of Wimbledon and many matches have been cancelled; but it's summer, and although everyone is hacked off with the weather most think it won't last much longer. They are obviously not listening to the long-term forecast.

This is my third visit back to England since I moved to Australia in 1981. Previous visits have been rushed; each time a few weeks spent racing from place to place, catching up with relatives, old friends and old places. But this is different; I have time to acclimatise, to explore this story slowly, and to indulge my longing for the England of my childhood. I am here for the past in more ways than one. I'm searching not simply for the Guinea Pigs and their nurses but for an England and a way of being English that began in the exhausted stasis of the immediate postwar years, through the slow recovery of the 50s, and on into the hope and energy of the first half of the 60s. That time—that England—is always linked in my memory to the presence of the Guinea Pigs. I want their stories, but I also want to find the essential nature of that England once again.

Bob Marchant is waiting for me under the clock at the entrance to the Queen Victoria Hospital. We have never met but as I park the car and run through the rain I can see him there, a small nuggetty man, with a fine head of silver hair, wearing a light raincoat. Now in his seventies, Marchant is too young to have been a Guinea Pig, but in the 1950s and early 60s he was McIndoe's theatre technician, at a time when many of those wartime patients were still returning regularly for treatment. Now he is the Honorary Secretary of the Guinea Pig Club, the keeper of the flame and the curator of the Guinea Pig Museum which exists entirely due to his voluntary effort to establish and maintain it single-handed.

'We might start off with the memorial,' Bob says, when we have done with the pleasantries. And he leads me down a long corridor that opens into a reception area where a roll of honour occupies one wall—a memorial to the men of the Guinea Pig Club. 'They're all there,' he says. 'British, Canadians, Australians, Czechs, Belgians, Poles, all of them.' We stand there briefly in the silence. Some of these names are well known: Richard Hillary, the Spitfire pilot and author of *The Last Enemy,* one of the most famous memoirs of WWII; Jimmy Wright who, despite losing his sight, managed to build a successful film company after the war; Bill Simpson, author of *One of Our Pilots is Safe* and *The Way of Recovery;* and Bill Foxley, who has the unenviable distinction of being the most severely burned airman to survive World War II. Others have published their own memoirs, have featured in books about the RAF, the Battle of Britain and in television documentaries. Some stories have endured while others have been swallowed up in the mists of the past.

'Why don't we talk over a cup of tea?' Bob says, and we set off through the rain, across the car park to the hospital café which is now located in the building that was once Ward III, 'The burns unit,' he says, 'where it all began.'

East Grinstead Cottage Hospital began life in a large old house called Green Hedges in 1863, and moved twice to larger houses until the construction of the present, purpose-built hospital in 1936. The name Queen Victoria Hospital was adopted some years later. We pause in front of the semi-circular, two-storey, red-brick building with its central curved entry topped with a column and a flagpole entwined by the snake of Asclepius, the Greek god of medicine. It is a fine building, characteristic of its era, its shape and scale a welcome change from contemporary sharp angles and multiple storeys. 'There were two twelve-bed wards, one for men and one for women, a six-bed ward for children, some private rooms and offices and an operating theatre,' Bob says. 'Perfect for its time, but not enough with war on the way.'

We move on, picking our way around the puddles until Bob grasps my arm to stop me. Looking around to check our position he points out that I'm standing with one foot in the eastern hemisphere, the other in the west, straddling the line of the Greenwich meridian that runs through the car park. All those years and I never knew that the meridian bisects the town. The confusion of my feelings about being back here after so long makes this bisection seem weirdly significant.

Many additions have been made to the hospital since its original construction, some of them immediately prior to and during the early years of the war. Faced with the prospect of war, the Ministry of Health acquired land adjacent to the hospital and erected three wooden army huts to accommodate an additional 120 beds. The children's ward was converted to a second operating theatre. Flagstone paths, covered overhead but open to the elements on both sides, linked the new wards.

'You need to remember that everyone who went into surgery had to be wheeled along this path to the operating theatre and back again, in all weathers,' Bob says, as we stand there copping the effects of a blustery wind that drives the rain in constantly changing directions. 'It wasn't an ideal arrangement.'

As a place where medical history was made and lives were transformed, Ward III comes as something of a shock to the modern visitor. It still looks like what it was – an army hut. Alongside the entrance is a commemorative plaque. A topiarist has clipped a small privet hedge into the just-recognisable shape of a winged guinea pig, the emblem of the club. It looks, at first glance, more like a rabbit, but it is a modest and moving memorial to the courage, endurance and spirit of the men who were treated here. Once inside, I find it hard to adjust to the fact that I am standing at the counter of a café, ordering tea and sandwiches, in the exact place where men once lay, their lives in the balance, their eyelids, noses and lips burned away, their fingers fused to shapeless webs, wondering about the possibilities of life and love after surviving the ravages of fire. Perhaps my own confusing emotional relationship to the time and place are making me oversensitive. I ask Bob why the ward was not preserved as a more fitting memorial, perhaps housing the Guinea Pig Museum. He shrugs and changes the subject. Maybe there is more history around this decision than he wants to discuss. It is only months later that I realise that despite a generalised commitment to the Guinea Pigs themselves, there has been only fragmented effort and limited finance allocated to the museum and it would likely not exist were it not for Bob Marchant's tireless custodianship over the years.

*

'It's a nice little hospital on the outskirts of a nice little town,' Archibald McIndoe wrote to his mother, the artist Mabel Hill, after his first visit to East Grinstead Cottage Hospital in mid-1939. 'I think something can be made of it.'[2]

It was the first of a series of visits since he had learned he was to be drafted there as a civilian consultant as part of the British Government's preparations for war. It was clear even then that fire would be a devastating force on the home front, as well as in the armed forces. There were, at the time, only four experienced plastic surgeons in the country and even the RAF, which had invested heavily in research on the fireproofing of its aircraft, had no real idea of the devastation it would wreak on its fliers. On that first and subsequent visits McIndoe had inspected the facilities with the team he had chosen from among his colleagues at St Bartholomew's Hospital: anaesthetist John Hunter, theatre sister Jill Mullins, and a young assistant surgeon, Percy Jayes.[3] A nice little hospital perhaps, but none of the team were impressed by what they saw—particularly Ward III—a long, low, wooden building that reeked of creosote, with a concrete floor, the walls painted in standard cream and brown. 'A bit of a shack,' McIndoe commented to Sister Jill Mullins who was to supervise nursing in the new ward. 'Still, we can probably tart it up a bit.'[4]

By September, McIndoe had developed an awkward and sometimes abrasive relationship with the hospital board. The minutes of its meeting on 4th September 1939 record that: 'Mr McIndoe has arrived to take over the Hospital on behalf of the Ministry of Health as a maxillo-facial hospital, although he has no written instructions.'[5] Whether that simple note is tinged with outrage or just bewilderment is not clear, but there is no doubt that the board was shaken by the arrival of the thirty-nine year old civilian consultant who seemed about to usurp its authority. As the board members and the staff struggled to get to grips with their new leader and his plans, none could have predicted the extent of the extraordinary and historic relationship that would develop and where it would lead. But the story of Archibald McIndoe and the Guinea Pigs begins a long time before he arrived at East Grinstead and long before the Royal Air Force began its preparations for war.

*

In 1925, Archibald McIndoe, at the age of twenty-five and from a strong Presbyterian background, was the first New Zealander to win a prestigious Fellowship with the Mayo Clinic in the USA, an institution widely acknowledged as being at the leading edge of developments in surgery at the time. His wife, Adonia, left her home in Dunedin, her family and her career as a pianist, to join him. McIndoe had already been singled out as an outstanding surgeon and he was developing a reputation there for stomach surgery. The couple planned for a future in America and applied for citizenship. It was while they waited to hear whether their application would be approved that Archie had a sudden and dramatic change of heart. Early in 1930, Berkeley George, Lord Moynihan, then president of the Royal College of Surgeons in England, paid a visit to the Mayo and saw McIndoe operate. There are several versions of what happened next but according to both McIndoe's biographers, Moynihan persuaded him that he was wasted at the Mayo. 'London's the place for you. I'm building a new hospital and you are the man I want,' Moynihan said. 'Sell up and come across the Atlantic. England needs young fellows like you.'[6]

Archie McIndoe was ambitious and single-minded in pursuit of what he wanted and now London was what he wanted, but Adonia had no desire to move. She loved their comfortable new home in Minnesota, the pleasant social life, and she had found work both at the Mayo and teaching the piano. The English climate and a lower standard of living held no appeal for her. It took Archie several months and a dastardly act of deception before she agreed to risk the move. As Adonia protested and procrastinated, the US citizenship papers finally arrived and, without her knowledge, Archie destroyed them. Only later, once they were settled in England, did he admit what he had done.[7]

The McIndoes arrived in London in November 1930 to discover a cold, damp city shrouded in fog; Adonia's worst fears were confirmed. In addition to the miserable weather, the British spirit was at its lowest, unemployment was high and there seemed no end in sight. The accommodation was appalling: '... the only lodging they could find to meet their budget was a furnished basement flat in Maida Vale where grease was thick on the walls and the lavatory smelled.'[8] Adonia was pregnant and all their hopes for a rapid improvement in the situation hung on Moynihan's promise of a job in the new hospital. But Moynihan proved hard to pin down. When McIndoe finally scored an appointment at His Lordship's Harley Street practice, Moynihan had no idea who he was. The new hospital was still on the drawing board and the job on which McIndoe had built his hopes simply didn't exist.

It seems extraordinary that in the seven months between meeting Moynihan at the Mayo and his own arrival in England, McIndoe had never once followed up the invitation or made any contact with him. Biographer Leonard Mosley suggests that the single-mindedness that would serve him and his patients so well during his time at East Grinstead, was also the force behind this risky move. One is, Mosley writes, 'driven to the conclusion that he did not write to Moynihan because he did not want to hear that the job did not exist.'

It was his excuse to get away from the slow and predictable process of advancement at the Mayo '... and he longed for an opportunity to branch out on his own.'[9]

But Archibald McIndoe was not unemployed for long. Before the end of that year he took up an appointment as a clinical assistant in the Department of Plastic Surgery at St Bartholomew's Hospital, and later became a general surgeon and lecturer in tropical medicine at the London School of Hygiene and Tropical Medicine. And he had family connections. His cousin Harold Gillies had built a significant reputation in plastic surgery, treating more than eleven thousand casualties of the Great War, and had established a special facility at the Queens Hospital in Sidcup. During and after the war Gillies had pushed out the boundaries of plastic surgery working with skin grafts on servicemen who were severely burned. His pioneering work had been rewarded with a knighthood.

While McIndoe was working at St Bartholomew's and the School of Tropical Medicine, Gillies encouraged him to develop his skills in plastic surgery by taking on some work in his practice. The challenge was considerable for a man with large square hands and thick blunt fingers which seemed entirely unsuited to the fine and delicate work of plastic surgery. But in the eight years that followed, McIndoe built a reputation in this new discipline and became a partner in the Gillies practice. He was working in an area that he believed had huge potential for the future, and while Adonia still struggled with life in England, Archie was convinced he had found his home and his speciality. By 1938 the McIndoes had two daughters, a substantial income, a comfortable rented home in Hampstead and grounds for believing that further advancement was just around the corner. But around that corner was the threat of war.

'If it's peace,' McIndoe told his brother, John, who visited him early in 1939, 'in ten years I shall be able to retire. If it is war, I'll be put in uniform and pushed around by Jacks-in-office. I've gambled on peace.'[10] But he had backed the wrong horse and he had no idea then how war would shape his work, his family life, his future career and reputation. Plastic surgery was still in its early days but great strides had been made and its role in wartime was to have unimaginable dimensions.

More than twenty years earlier, as the wounded from the First World War had flowed into hospitals, Harold Gillies and his contemporaries had been faced for the first time with casualties of war in the air. These men had suffered severe burns when the petrol tanks of their aircraft exploded in flames under enemy fire. Hasty efforts were made to redesign and relocate the fuel tanks on some aircraft but it was small protection against the universally feared effects of burning fuel that the pilots came to call 'the orange death'.[11] The injuries were horrific and usually deadly. But the pilots were not alone in their facial disfigurement. More than sixty thousand men were either shot in the head or eye, or wounded by flying, burning debris. Thousands were rendered unrecognisable, their faces so horrifying they were abandoned by wives, girlfriends and family members who could not accept the disfigurement.

The only solution seemed to lie in full or partial facemasks to hide the loss of jawbones, noses, chins, eyes and cheeks. Artists and surgeons collaborated in the construction of masks made of extremely fine copper shaped from a cast made of the injured face. The copper was then coated with enamel to match the man's skin tone, the features tinted with paint using fine brushes. But the masks, while initially realistic, lacked any of the frequently changing and nuanced expressions of the human face, an effect that proved as alienating in the long-term as the reality of the disfigured face. And while men could claim government compensation of sixteen shillings a week for the loss of a limb, there was no compensation for injuries above the neck. Eyes, noses, chins, ears, even whole faces mashed beyond recognition, were treated as worthless, and in the wider community facial disfigurement was often assumed to be associated with mental illness and was met with fear and mistrust. Thousands were confined in miserable conditions in homes for the blind, or discarded and left to beg on the streets.

At Sidcup, Gillies had experimented with new surgical

procedures to replace missing noses and chins, and to fill eye sockets, often performing multiple operations over a period of time to reconstruct the face, combining art with surgery by drawing the reconstruction based on pre-war photographs of the patient. His work was slow and produced varying results but he was crafting a new direction in plastic surgery which would lead the profession into the next conflagration. Research between the wars meant that by 1930, solutions had been found that would counter the burns victim's worst enemy—the catastrophic effects of shock that drained fluid from the wound site, and created secondary shock as the body struggled to redistribute fluid to vital organs. The body's chemical balance could be restored by combining plasma with saline treatments in larger quantities than previously thought possible. It meant that patients who would, in the past, have died within the first twenty-four hours could now expect to live.[12] But neither this nor the development of reconstructive surgery prepared the medical profession for the numbers of patients or the extent of the horrific injuries that another war would deliver to their doors.

Following his first visit, McIndoe had organised the repainting of Ward III in lighter, more cheerful colours. He had the regulation beds and metal lockers replaced with furnishings more reminiscent of a suburban home than a hospital ward. The first patients arrived to an environment that was a rarity for its time. Meanwhile, by the time war was declared in September 1939, the board's budget was diminishing at an alarming rate, as was the surgeon's personal financial status. McIndoe had been paying off by instalments the cost of his share in Gillies' practice and, while financially comfortable, the McIndoes' only assets were their household goods and a Rolls Royce that Archie had bought when he was gambling on peace. Nineteen thirty-nine was to have been the turning point at which he expected to see the financial rewards of his work and ultimately to buy a cottage in the South of France where he, Adonia and the children could escape from the worst excesses of the English climate. But now he was working for the RAF. He had been offered a commission as

Wing Commander, a comparatively junior rank that he felt would not afford him the status he wanted and needed for the job. He opted instead to remain a civilian, believing that it would give him more freedom and independence than he would have within the service. It was a decision that was to prove prescient in the coming months, but did nothing to improve his domestic or financial situation in the short term. He had embarked on a new phase of life forced on him by the war and neither he, his family, his close colleagues nor his future staff could have had any idea that they were all about to be participants in a therapeutic experiment that would become a landmark in medical history and influence the treatment of burns patients into a new century.

3. PREPARATIONS FOR WAR

Several days after my visit to the hospital, I watch the coverage of Tony Blair departing Downing Street for Buckingham Palace in an armour-plated car, to deliver his resignation to the Queen and, sometime later, the arrival at the palace of a tense and awkward-looking Gordon Brown. The long and rancorous 'marriage of convenience' is over. 'Teflon Tony' is out, and a country exhausted by charisma and spin waits with trepidation for a very different sort of Labour prime minister to establish himself.

For many, myself included, Gordon Brown comes as a relief. He exudes a quiet, occasionally morose sort of substance and authority. He is more 50s than flash, more interiority than performance, an apparently dull but safe pair of hands. According to the commentators, his manner leaves much to be desired; in a world obsessed with celebrity performance Gordon turns away at all the wrong moments, struggles to smile when he should beam, mumbles something cryptic when a joke is called for. Around the country people are waiting to see if he can shake off this carapace and win the hearts and minds. Time will tell.

The rain has stopped, giving way a few days ago to early summer sunshine. Nostalgia constantly takes me by surprise with images of the past that overlay the present: my father steps out of the Midland Bank tucking his wallet into his inside pocket and turning to cross the road. Through the window of the shoe shop I see my mother stretch out her leg, tilting her foot to inspect a black suede court shoe. I pause outside what is now a jeweller's shop, remembering that this was once Walton's, the greengrocer, where Mum bought fruit and vegetables from tall moustachioed man in a brown overall, with a ready smile and terrible alopecia. I pass a bus stop and see myself, small, aged perhaps nine or ten, alone, dressed in an ugly, brown school uniform and beret, shifting nervously from one foot to the other, praying that the bus will come before the older boys from the nearby grammar school pour out at the final bell in time to tease me.

I'm staying in a small studio in the grounds of a beautiful old house on the outskirts of the village of Hartfield, just five miles outside East Grinstead. In many ways it is similar to Copthorne, the village where I grew up and which is a similar distance from the town, but in the opposite direction. I've rented the studio for the duration of my stay. It is perfect: compact, cosy and filled with natural light. On one level there is a tiny bathroom and kitchen that reminds me of the galley on a yacht, and a bedroom/study area, from which four steps lead down to a large lounge with comfy chairs, a sofa and television. I ended up here with the help of Simon Kerr, who manages tourism for the East Grinstead Council, from an office in the local library where his wife Susie is the librarian. We first met a year ago on email when Simon and Susie came across one of my novels, in which some scenes are set in East Grinstead and Simon emailed to ask if I knew the town. We soon discovered that all three of us are of a similar age, and spent our youth in or near the town. We discovered so many coincidences and connections between us, both here and, surprisingly, in Perth, that it feels as though we have almost brushed shoulders many times throughout our lives. When I told Simon that I was planning a long visit to write a book about the Guinea Pigs and needed somewhere to stay, he sent me information about this studio, owned by his friends Malcolm and Barbara.

It feels like pure bliss to be here in the Sussex countryside, in this glorious English garden, reminiscent of the garden of my childhood home, and tucked away a mile or more from the main road, along a narrow lane. Malcolm and Barbara have made me welcome, but also left me, as I had hoped, to my own devices. Now they have left for a holiday in France, encouraging me to pick and eat the raspberries that are hanging heavily from the canes, and gather the early roses, as I wonder how I will ever get to grips with the project which seems so much more complex now than when I imagined it back home in Australia.

Hartfield is Winnie the Pooh Country, perched at the edge of one of England's best-kept secrets, Ashdown Forest, often mentioned but rarely featured in tourist guides. It is part of the High Weald, an area of 560 square miles spanning East and West Sussex, Surrey and Kent. In Norman times the ten square miles of the forest itself was deer-hunting country. Later Henry VIII had a hunting lodge here and courted Anne Boleyn at nearby Hever Castle. Today the forest is the largest public access open space in England, a mix of dense woodland, sweeping grasslands, and lowland heath covered with purple heather, dazzling yellow gorse and, in spring, dense patches of bluebells. The deer hunting is, thankfully, long gone but the deer, four species of them, remain along with some rogue sheep, and a wide variety of birds and small wildlife and, of course, the spirit of Winnie the Pooh.

Since that first visit to the hospital in the pouring rain, I have spent hours in the Guinea Pig Museum reading through the decades of newspaper cuttings that Bob Marchant has so faithfully collected and mounted in a series of albums. I have read the stories of McIndoe's patients and studied the stages of repair and reconstruction of their faces recorded in hospital photographs. I've held the surgical instruments that McIndoe designed and had manufactured for use in the hospital, studied the wax models of jaw reconstruction, and the pictures of groups of men in uniform—their faces and hands in various stages of treatment, or grouped around their Maestro as he plays the piano. I've searched the photographs for a glimpse of the man at the foot of the stairs, but he has eluded me. And I've driven to a high point in the forest, originally called Gill's Lap, to walk through the wooded and the open parts of the forest and wallow in the memories it evokes. This is the England of my childhood and, despite six decades, it is surprisingly, reassuringly unchanged.

In the final chapter of the Pooh books author A. A. Milne

renamed Gills Lap 'Galleons Leap', but today it is better known as the Enchanted Place—the place where Pooh and Christopher Robin take their last walk together. Christopher Robin is going away; no one knows where he is going or why, but they know it is an ending and that in future 'Things are going to be Different.' Rabbit has called a meeting at which Eeyore makes a speech announcing that he and Pooh, 'a Bear with a Pleasing Manner but a Positively Startling Lack of Brain', have written a new poem. It is a goodbye poem for Christopher Robin, and when it has been read and everyone has clapped and the goodbyes have been said, Christopher Robin and Pooh walk to 'that enchanted place on the very top of the forest called Galleons Leap'.[13] It is an iconic spot for Pooh tragics like me who grew up with the Bear of Little Brain and his friends. I keep returning here to gaze out over the broad meadows, robust hedgerows, the spires, the scattered farms and undulating Sussex hills, the swelling strains of an Elgar symphony playing in my head, and wondering where I really belong.

McIndoe loved this forest. When it became clear that he would need a home near the hospital, he rented Little Warren, a cottage on its border. This was his home throughout the war years. It is barely visible from the road but I park outside staring at the dense hedge, wondering about this man who staked everything on a move from New Zealand to America, only to throw it all in on a vague suggestion from someone he barely knew. He had turned that risky move into success and with what he had learned from working with Gillies, he was anticipating a stellar career in a developing speciality. He believed totally in the therapeutic value of plastic surgery. Whether it was a socialite or film star who wanted her nose remodelled, a woman struggling with pendulous breasts, a child with a cleft palate or hare lip, or a patient with burns, facial fractures, or damage from another surgeon's knife, he was in the business of making people look better and, more importantly, making them feel better about themselves. He already numbered some significant names among his patients and his reputation, particularly for the 'McIndoe Nose', was spreading by word of mouth. But the war ended all that, putting his material aspirations and his future career on hold, leaving him irritable and frustrated.

On his early visits to East Grinstead, McIndoe had delivered lectures to nurses on the nature of plastic surgery and the methods he would be using, and he had spoken at length about the need to empathise with the patients and develop an insight into their psychological condition. Some nurses found him exciting and looked forward to the time when he would take up his appointment, while others were intimidated by his brusque manner. In those early days, McIndoe was always well turned out. His thick, dark hair was severely parted in the middle and glossy with Brylcreem and he favoured pinstriped suits, often with a carnation in his lapel, and wore round and heavy-rimmed bifocals. As time passed and war filled the hospital wards, he reverted to a baggy sports jacket and cords. He was not handsome, but photographs suggest a fine-looking man of enormous self-confidence. And there was never any shortage of women who were attracted to him. He had established a home for himself close to the hospital, but Adonia and their daughters, Adonia junior and Vanora, stayed on in London, where the girls were at an expensive private school. The McIndoes were struggling to pay the rent on two homes and Archie himself was anxious about the family's safety. Throughout the months of the Phoney War the possibility of enemy attacks on London was on most people's minds. Friends and former colleagues at the Mayo had offered accommodation for Adonia and the girls but Adonia, who was by now settled in London, refused to leave. Along with the financial pressure, the emotional pressure also increased until, early in 1940, she finally agreed and left with their daughters for Minnesota, leaving Archie free to throw all his efforts into the task ahead.[14]

Over the next few years of working twelve to sixteen hours a day in the operating theatre, proximity to the forest provided McIndoe with moments of peace and relaxation. He walked here often and one corner of the forest later acquired a special meaning for him. The Airman's Grave is a memorial to the six-man crew of a Wellington bomber of 142 Squadron who were killed when it crashed in the forest on the morning of 31st July 1941 on its return from a raid on Cologne. The memorial, a simple stone-walled enclosure on the heathland, shelters a white cross surrounded by a tiny garden of remembrance and was erected by the mother of Sergeant P. V. R. Sutton, who was aged twenty-four at the time of his death. Each year a short memorial service is held here on Remembrance Sunday. These days an Ashdown Forest ranger lays the wreath, but during the war years McIndoe laid it once at the personal request of Mrs Sutton.

*

In 1939, as McIndoe and the staff of the Queen Victoria Hospital prepared for war, others who would ultimately end up in East Grinstead were making their own preparations.

In Brighton, Alice*, aged seventeen, won a battle of several months, when her parents agreed to let her volunteer as a VAD.

Eighteen-year-old Jack Toper was bursting to do something useful, and excited at the prospect of learning to fly.

Sixteen-year-old Joyce* had left her East London school, and was working part-time in a local draper's shop and helping her widowed mother to look after her five younger siblings.

Dennis Neale, had joined the RAF at the age of fifteen and now, four years later, was assigned to Bomber Command.

In Liverpool, Bill Foxley celebrated his sixteenth birthday and 'thought a lot about girls'.

Bridget Warner, aged twenty, was scrubbing, sterilising, preparing dressings and emptying bedpans, as a trainee nurse in Southampton.

In Stockport, Alan Morgan, a seventeen-year-old apprentice toolmaker, had already met the love of his life and was planning to enlist in the navy.

And on the morning that war was declared, Richard Hillary, the best known and least typical of those who would become 'McIndoe's boys', was at his parents' home in Beaconsfield, listening to Prime Minister Neville Chamberlain's broadcast.

Hillary was two years into his degree at Trinity College, Oxford, and had also joined the University Air Squadron that provided free training to would-be flyers, at government expense. Later that day he drove to Squadron headquarters in Oxford and was assigned to lead a platoon of undergraduates. A month later he was called up into the RAF.

None of these, nor any of the hundreds more who would end up as staff or patients at East Grinstead in the next few years, could have had any sense of what the war, the town and the hospital had in store for them.

4. THE BURNING QUESTION

During the first months of the Phoney War, life at East Grinstead was relatively quiet. It was December 1939 before the first RAF pilot arrived with burns to his face and back. But it was in March 1940 that McIndoe was first faced with the horrific reality of what was ahead. He was making regular rounds of the other RAF hospitals, and at Halton saw a young pilot, Godfrey Edmonds, whose entire face had been burned away when he crashed his aircraft on a training flight. McIndoe ordered his immediate transfer to East Grinstead. The challenge was daunting, even for this tough and confident surgeon. Emily Mayhew writes that 'Edmonds was the first East Grinstead patient to require more than twenty operations to restore his face, after which he returned to flying and then to training some of the early paratroops.'[15] McIndoe's shock was two-fold: not only was he faced with the worst case of facial burns he'd seen, but with the reality of a patient who, some years earlier, would not have survived. But even Gillies's groundbreaking work in plastics could go only a small part of the way to reconstructing faces and hands so devastatingly destroyed by the fire. Years later McIndoe told his friend, the actor Angela Fox, that until then he had known he 'was a good, competent and experienced surgeon, but when I looked at a burned boy for the first time and saw that I must replace his eyelids, God came down my right arm.'[16]

The evacuation from Dunkirk began on 26th May and by 4th June, 364,628 troops—eighty-five per cent of the British Expeditionary Force—had been rescued and brought home. In Germany, Goering was urging an immediate invasion to take advantage of losses of personnel and morale and the exhaustion of the troops. But Hitler had different priorities and the action that might have ended the war in Germany's favour was delayed. At home, Churchill was urging Britons to fight on, but he was up against those who urged a pact with Germany as preferable to the risk of invasion. But Churchill would not compromise. In a speech on 18th June he insisted that the Battle for France was over, and he anticipated that the Battle for Britain was about to begin. Just three weeks later he was proved prescient when radar plotters stationed on the cliffs of Dover picked up blips that indicated seventy enemy aircraft were heading for a naval convoy that was travelling westward with a guard escort of six Hurricane fighters. It was the start of a battle in the skies over a stretch of the English Channel that came to be known as Hellfire Corner. Britain lost fifty aircraft and shot down ninety-two Luftwaffe planes. Six RAF pilots died in one day alone and the wounded began to arrive in RAF hospitals. Soon McIndoe and his staff would walk out onto the hospital lawns and watch the extraordinary spectacle of the war being fought in the air over south-east England, knowing that they would soon be treating some of its casualties.

Burned flyers from both Fighter and Bomber Command were arriving in the RAF hospitals in horrifying numbers. The fighter pilots' injuries mapped a pattern of burns that reflected the design of the aircraft. The cockpit was located above and behind the main fuel tanks. When these were hit by enemy fire they exploded, enveloping the face, head, neck, hands and the front and insides of the thighs. Pilots were issued with helmets, goggles and gauntlets for protection, but these, particularly the goggles and gloves, were constricting and awkward in the confined space of the cockpit, and the men frequently removed them. The intensity of the fire created deep and incapacitating wounds to all areas, particularly the face and hands, a condition that came to be known as 'airman's burn'. While the deepest wounds are the least painful because the nerve endings are destroyed they also present the greatest challenge of reconstruction and repair. Mayhew describes the extent of these devastating 'whole thickness' burns. 'Whole thickness burns are the most serious of all, where all skin and tissue is destroyed, including sebaceous glands, hair follicles, sweat glands and nerve endings.'[17]

Until now the traditional treatment of burns involved the use of coagulants and, in particular, tannic acid, a 'leathering' agent used in tanneries. Coagulants were relatively easily applied to wounds and formed a hard shell that sealed the area, protecting it from infection. Packed in a sealed tube, Tannafax jelly was easy to transport and seemed ideally suited for application in the field. But 'the field' was not the sterile environment of a hospital and in some cases the coagulant was applied over hair or already infected skin, allowing infections to develop unobserved. But there were other major problems with coagulants. Gillies, McIndoe and their partners had been seeking ways to treat burns while preserving the stability of the wound site as the foundation from which to reconstruct the face. Treating the face with tannic acid led to horrific scarring, and often to blindness, because when this, or gentian violet, was used around the eyes, the skin stiffened and the eyelids shrank back, leaving corneas exposed and subject to thickening. The hands also suffered when coagulants were painted around the fingers. Fingertips became fused together or fused onto palms and the soft skin between the fingers thickened to form webs. The remaining tissue developed 'rope-like scars out of all proportion to the trauma site ... which pulled the fingers back into a kind of frozen claw.'[18] McIndoe knew he had to find another method of treating burns—a method that would not make an already disastrous situation even worse.

In his search for a solution to the problem of coagulants and the need to preserve the viability of the burned area, McIndoe introduced soft, loosely woven dressings impregnated with Vaseline jelly. Tulle gras—curtain netting cutting into squares—was most commonly used and the dressings, made up in advance, were stored in sterile containers. It was a high-maintenance system compared to a handy tube of coagulant but it kept the wounds moist and soft. The worst part of the day in any burns ward is when the dressings are changed, and it is never pain free, but these were a marked improvement over the ripping, chipping agony of coagulant shells, that men described as far more agonising than the original burns. And the light moist dressing largely maintained the viability of the burned area.

McIndoe had realised that the men who came down in the sea fared better than those who crashed on land and that too took him back to basics. He introduced saline baths to the ward. The warm salt water allowed the dressings to float away and patients to gently move their injured hands and limbs, and keep their wounds flexible. It was successful but labour intensive as patients often needed two or more baths each day. The first saline bath was of standard design with hot and cold taps and the salt added by hand. But getting in and out was difficult for the men who sometimes injured themselves on the taps. Before long they were removed and the salt water, just above body temperature, was piped into the bath through pipes connected to a tank located in the roof of the ward.

The success of this new treatment was evident and McIndoe soon mounted a campaign to stop the use of coagulants. By the end of 1940 not only the RAF but the Ministry of Health had issued orders stating that burns should be treated with open irrigation techniques and the use of coagulants was abandoned. It was a crucial victory for burns patients and for McIndoe's status and reputation, which he would go on to use in future battles with those and other hierarchies. McIndoe's reputation as a surgeon, his innovative approach to surgery, and his determination to fight for his patients was spreading. There would be more battles with officialdom to come, and in most cases his belief in what he was doing and what he wanted, together with his stamina, would win the day.

5. FACE TO FACE

It's almost five weeks since I arrived here and I haven't yet met a Guinea Pig. Bob Marchant, having decided that I am serious and apparently trustworthy, has promised to contact some who may be willing to talk to me. In the meantime I wait impatiently for his call, scanning the newspaper archives in the local library, and filling time wondering how I will begin to find the nurses. It has started raining again. The Met Office has predicted more to come with additional flooding in already saturated areas. All due, apparently, to La Nina in the Pacific Ocean, and the jet stream being further south than usual. There were massive disruptions to Saturday's matches at Wimbledon. Here in Sussex the rain continues with long dry periods, and so far no floods. I mark time by taking the train to London and spending a couple of days in the reading room at the Imperial War Museum.

I am searching for personal accounts of women who either nursed on Ward III, or who were encouraged by McIndoe to do voluntary work at the hospital. Unlike the Guinea Pigs who have a solid network and a mailing list, there is no network for the nurses. While some may have been local women, the rest could have been recruited from, or drafted to, East Grinstead from anywhere in the country. The helpful librarian-archivist at the College of Nursing tells me there are no records in their archives. I have great hopes of the Imperial War Museum where a couple of file numbers sound promising, but when the files are brought to me they are disappointing. They are just short extracts of memoir containing facts I already know, no revelations of personal experience. What I do find though is a long and very detailed memoir of a woman who nursed a burned serviceman in the nearby hospital at Tunbridge Wells, before he was transferred to McIndoe's care at East Grinstead. And there's another by a woman whose mother volunteered her as a dance partner at a party organised by McIndoe for his patients in 1942. I take copious notes and search for other leads, struggling with the torpor induced by the airlessness of the reading room, and the feeling that I am getting nowhere.

The train home to East Grinstead stops frequently between stations for no explicable reason, and we passengers sit in weird, uncomfortable silence waiting for it to start again. I remember similar journeys on this line, sitting opposite my mother as a child, a teenager, a young woman. What would she think of this adventure into the past? Not much I suspect. She disliked the idea of anything that involved poking one's nose into other people's business. Her fear of disapproval, of seeming intrusive or inappropriate, of being a nuisance, would have made her very uneasy with the purpose of my visit. I did a lot of things she disapproved of, and I suspect she guessed that there were many more that would have horrified her had she known about them. But as I have aged I have come to realise that, in her own quiet way, she admired my difference, my resistance, sometimes perhaps even envied it. I feel her presence strongly in this silent train, parked between steep, grass-covered banks, speckled with cow parsley. Indeed, she has been looking over my shoulder since I got here, reminding me of how I'm supposed to behave. Sometimes I swear I can hear her sharp intake of breath when I cross a line. My mother died more than a decade ago. I still think of her every day, and I still miss her, but here in England, in this train, and in lanes and streets where we walked together, beneath trees whose shade we once shared, in such a different life, I miss her more acutely than ever.

The train gives a jolt, and then another. We passengers shift our positions, hopeful of progress. Slowly it begins to move on, and I hear my phone buzzing in my handbag.

'What are you doing on Wednesday?' Bob Marchant asks.

*

At 12.30 pm on Wednesday I am standing in the lobby at the Felbridge Hotel, an MP3 recorder strung around my neck, a notebook in my bag, half an hour early for my appointment with Jack Toper who, for the last four years, has been the Chairman of the Guinea Pig Club, and has edited its magazine since the 70s. In the days when this hotel was known as Ye Olde Felbridge, its bar was a favourite with McIndoe's 'boys', and they still return to celebrate their anniversary with a dinner here. But, now in their eighties, this year will be the last for the remaining few. To mark the occasion the club's President, His Royal Highness Prince Philip, will attend. Jack Toper is coming here today to talk security arrangements with the hotel management. But first, thanks to Bob Marchant, he's going to talk to me.

Jack Toper's face is familiar—it is one of the most photographed of the Guinea Pig faces captured at various stages of reconstruction: the young wireless operator with a big smile sporting a leather flying jacket and helmet; then Jack the burns victim, his face a distorted mass of burned tissue; and later, on Ward III with his right arm strapped across his chest to his opposite shoulder and tethered, by what looks like a trunk, to the place where his nose used to be. This trunk is McIndoe's tubular pedicle, developed from initial efforts by Harold Gillies in the First War. The pedicle is a flap of skin raised from the soft flesh of the inner arm or the chest where one end remains attached while the other is cut and the flap rolled and stitched into a tube and attached to the face for up to eight weeks. There the pedicle is nourished by blood circulating in the live tissue of the arm until new flesh is sufficiently well established for the pedicle to be cut away and the flesh shaped into a nose, a chin or a cheek. In the next photograph, Jack's pedicle has gone and in the centre of his face is a fleshy lump soon to be built up with pig gristle to look and work as a nose. And then the present day Jack—no longer the stuff of childhood nightmares—a smiling eighty-six year-old face, with a strong nose, broad and shiny lips, scarred and stretched skin, but no longer hideously disfigured. As the owner of that face walks into the hotel lobby the first thing I notice is not his face at all, but his presence: a man of medium height who walks tall, a man with a warm and open manner and a modest but unmistakeable air of authority.

'I was so excited when I went to sign up,' Jack tells me. 'I wanted to fly and frankly I never gave a thought to the danger. Most of us felt the same. As you climbed into those planes there was some apprehension but not real fear. I never thought that I might not come back.'

In August 1943, Jack Toper, then twenty-two, was the wireless operator on a 166 Squadron Wellington bomber. It was Jack's sixth raid and the flight was returning from its mission to drop incendiaries on Mönchengladbach when the starboard engine blew, sending them into a dramatic spin. The pilot managed to recover from the sudden loss of height within a few minutes and they limped back towards the North Sea heading for home.

'We were close to the coast when we were suddenly caught in the searchlights and that's a terrible feeling because you're just there—totally exposed,' Jack says. The pilot, Pat Knight, took evasive action and they got away but further evasive tactics were needed to get past the enemy's coastal defences. Knight took the Wellington down to just above sea level where the crew jettisoned everything. They crossed the English coast at Clacton-on-Sea and landed in a field where they hit a tree.

'The others bailed out, but someone had forgotten to jettison a parachute,' Jack explains. 'It opened and blocked my exit. I was trapped inside and as I struggled to get out, the line of oxygen tanks blew up in my face.' Jack fought his way out of the furnace, eventually emerging from the burning wreck. People who saw him described him as like a living candle, his face was on fire and six-foot flames shot up from it into the sky.

'Burning,' he says now, 'is such a strange thing. It's so fast you almost don't know it's happening. I lost my nose, my upper eyelids, the top of my right ear, my upper lip, the bottom of my chin and my right cheek—apart from that I was normal,' he laughs. 'And now here I am, a good-looking old bloke – aren't I?' And indeed he is. Time has transformed disfigurement into character, lurid colour to subtle weathering. Recent photographs indicate that age has been kind to many of these men, but that has come at a cost. It took twenty-six operations to rebuild Jack Toper's face; many of the club members had thirty, fifty or more visits to McIndoe's slab.

'Archie was not only an extraordinarily inspired surgeon, he was a wonderful person. It wasn't enough for him that he rebuilt our faces and hands,' Jack says. 'He wanted more than that for us. He wanted us to cope with facing other people, and being part of the world. He believed it would give us the will to live. More than anything he told us that the way we would get through it all was by sticking together, supporting each other, not only there in the hospital, but beyond that. He gave us faith in the future, and when you have faith you can live and come to terms with what's happened to you.' He rubs his nose. 'Archie gave me a good nose, but he did the pedicle process in stages, taking skin from a hairy place on my stomach, so now I have to shave my nose every two or three days. But that's only a small part of what he did. Human beings can adjust to anything if they are given the right sort of environment, that's what he gave us. We had a safe place to learn how to live again, and to discover who we were going to be at the end of all that.' Jack's hands were also severely burned and McIndoe worked on those, sculpting the remains of his fingers into usable stumps.

We talk about the Guinea Pig Club, how it began and how it grew from a drinking club to become a patient support group and then a welfare body that has supported the men in diverse ways through the postwar years and into a new century. 'Many wouldn't have survived without it,' Jack says. 'The world outside the hospital, outside East Grinstead, was a cruel one for people who looked like us.'

Neville and Elaine Blond, in their wartime tenancy at Saint Hill Manor, not only welcomed the Guinea Pigs into their homes to convalesce but also assisted in McIndoe's plan to get the men back into active service and postwar employment.

Elaine Blond was the sister of Sir Simon Marks, founder of Marks & Spencer, and Neville Blond was a member of the board.

'After the war I was able to get a job with M and S,' Jack says. 'I couldn't believe my luck, but I wanted to work in the stores, I wanted to train to be a manager. But they were afraid I would frighten the customers and so I was sent to the head office in Baker Street. I was told I couldn't have any contact with the public. That was very hard to take and Archie encouraged me to fight it. With his backing, the management agreed that I could do six weeks training on the shop floor and see how it went. Well, the customers and I survived. It was tough though: I had to get used to people staring at me, and to kids either shouting abuse or being terrified of me. But I stuck it out and became manager of the Camden Town store and spent the rest of my working life with the company. The outside world was hard for all of us. Archie turned the hospital and the town into a place where we were at home; people didn't stare, or point and they didn't turn away, but everywhere else it was hard to get used to what people said and did when they saw you.'

He gets to his feet, ready to move on to his meeting. 'Bob told me your father worked for M and S,' he says. 'I remember meeting him, but I can't say I knew him. Good credentials though.' He turns away, then back again. 'I wouldn't change it. If I could go back, I wouldn't change it. I would rather have gone through this than not be a Guinea Pig, it's been the centre of my life.'

Jack's words lodge in my mind. Surely it's just a figure of speech. Surely he can't mean that he would choose to relive the trauma that turned him into a living candle and have his face and hands burned away, to go through months of agonising treatments and twenty-six operations to not having been one of McIndoe's Guinea Pigs? But in the weeks to come I will hear others say the same thing, use the same language and say it with same almost imperceptible crack in their voices, and each time it will bring a lump to my throat, and fill me with a treacherous sense of unease.

6. AT THE PUB

Delving into childhood fears is like taking an opener to a rusty tin can. Each twist makes a cut and from each cut leaks the juice of memory. Sometimes it is pin sharp, more often it is contaminated with confused and shifting images. In a recurring dream I am standing alone in Blackwell Hollow wearing the party dress my mother has made for my birthday: white flocked organza with a turquoise satin sash. I am pressed against the damp rocks, knowing Mum will be furious if I get moss stains on the dress, but I dare not move. The men with the terrible faces are hiding in the trees. At last I break from the darkness and run home, in through the front door and up the stairs but outside my bedroom door one of them is waiting. The dream recurs constantly throughout my childhood, lessening in frequency as I reach my teens, but it's always there, even now. It never goes away.

Today I turn the car off the sunlit street and into the shadows of Blackwell Hollow, shivering at the sense of being swallowed into the darkness. This is how I felt as a child, as the bus made its way through this long archway of trees; through the shadows, the faces, the fear. Why, when I can now meet those men face to face, can I still not shake off their ghosts from the past?

I emerge again into sunlight and head out of town towards Crawley, to a pub called The Hedgehog. It's a couple of weeks or so since I met Jack Toper and I've interviewed five more of McIndoe's boys since then. Now I'm on my way to join a group of them at the pub where they meet for their twice-weekly pint, or several. The Hedgehog has other memories for me as I lived not far from it and spent many evenings and Sunday mornings here, drinking lager and lime with various boyfriends. In those days the drinking crowd were the Young Conservatives, not something I often admit to these days having been liberated into socialism by the protest movements of the late 60s. And I'm edgy; I've become something of a loner and am ill at ease meeting a bunch of strangers, so as I park my car and walk towards the lounge bar I wonder how well I'll fare with these new drinking companions.

I need not have worried. I doubt there is a collective noun for a group of Guinea Pigs, but I am about to encounter the collective energy, a present day version of that which must have pervaded Ward III and filled the East Grinstead pubs with laughter and ribaldry in the 1940s. These guys are in their eighties and I'm in my sixties, but the boys of the Young Conservatives couldn't hold a candle to the fast patter, the jokes, the tall tales and flirtatiousness of this band of Guinea Pigs. I end up sitting next to Tommy Brandon, who tells me that he was an air-gunner, and was burned when his Halifax crashed and exploded on landing. His injuries are not as extensive as those of some of the others, and his scars although visible have blended remarkably well into his overall appearance. His treatment in Ward III, he tells me, changed his life, determining his future career.

'It was the photographs that did it for me,' he says. 'Everyone who ended up at East Grinstead was photographed when they arrived and during the treatment. And The Boss always asked for photographs from before they were burned. It helped him to see how they'd looked then, and he'd try to get as close as he could to that. I understood how important the photographs were and I made up my mind to be a photographer when the war was over.' Shortly after the war Tommy trained as a medical photographer and later became the senior medical photographer at St Thomas's Hospital in London.

On my left is the legendary Bill Foxley, dapper in a pink shirt, cream linen jacket and his trademark dark glasses. Bill is one of the best known of the Guinea Pigs for his status as the most severely burned airman to survive the war. He was born in Liverpool and grew up in Thornton, now part of the

City of Bradford in West Yorkshire, home of the Brontës who are the town's most famous residents, followed closely by Bill. He joined the RAF in 1942 aged eighteen and trained as a navigator. He had just turned twenty when on 16th March 1944 he took off from Castle Donington on a training flight in a Wellington Bomber with five other crewmates. Almost immediately after take-off, at two hundred feet, the flaps suddenly dropped downward, causing the nose of the aircraft to pitch up. The Wellington stalled and crashed, bursting into flames.

'I managed to climb out through the astrodome,' Bill tells me, 'but I heard screaming and realised some of the others were still trapped.'

He turned back and found the wireless operator was still inside the burning fuselage, screaming for help. Bill struggled to free him but the man died, along with two other crew members. Bill was eventually dragged from the wreck and taken to hospital with potentially fatal third-degree burns. After that, he says, he can't remember much except lying in a hospital bed completely covered in bandages. The fire destroyed all the skin, muscle and cartilage up to his eyebrows, he had completely lost his right eye, and the cornea of the left eye was severely damaged, leaving him with dramatically impaired vision.

'Archie could only save one eye, but he gave me new eyelids, a great nose, lips and cheeks.' He holds up hands with finger stumps that extend less than half an inch beyond the knuckle. 'He separated my fingers and thumbs. They were just webs but Archie made them into something I can use.'

Apart from being able to blink with his McIndoe-issue eyelids, Bill can also move his mouth to eat and speak, but his face is expressionless as the muscles were completely destroyed in the fire. Even so, the warmth, the humour and compassion still shine through, transcending the scar tissue and grafts of almost thirty operations. His face is less weathered, pinker and seemingly more vulnerable than the others. It is not a handsome face, but he has the grace and style of a young Fred Astaire. When he removes his sunglasses his beautifully crafted glass eye seems to twinkle with life.

'Not so long ago, I lost my glass eye in Sainsbury's,' he says. 'It dropped down and rolled under the check-out counter and the girl had to crawl around and find it. If I lose it today will you find it for me?'

Bill's face and hands were repaired and rebuilt in twenty-nine operations over three and a half years. In 1947 he married Catherine Arkell, who worked in the hospital treasurer's office. After the war, when he was fully recovered, he decided that although there was little more that could be done to his face he could get his body into great shape. He began a rigorous program of athletic training to prove just how fit a Guinea Pig could be, and developed a reputation as a runner. Bill and Catherine were together until she died in 1971. He married again some years later and has a daughter and two sons from his second marriage. In 1969 Bill was cast in the role of a pilot with facial burns in the movie *Battle of Britain,* starring Kenneth More and Susannah York.

'It's personality that matters,' he says when I ask him how he has coped over the years, 'that's what gets you through it. You just have to get on with it. It took a very long time for other people to get over it—get over how I look. Years later, when I used to go to London on the train every day, people would get in the carriage and go to sit down beside me and they'd look at me and then move away. There'd always be an empty seat alongside me. Sometimes I ignored it, but sometimes I'd say, "It's all right, I don't bite."'

Now, twice widowed, he lives alone and does everything for himself except drive. 'I cook, I clean, I go dancing,' he says. 'And I'm still a glamour boy aren't I?'

Bill's pre-war best friend, Ray Brook, has driven him here today. The two men first met in 1942 when they began their training, but were then separated until they met up again in East Grinstead.

Ray was off-duty in Lancashire in August 1944 when a US B-24 bomber on a test flight crashed into a café where he was sheltering from the rain. 'I was with three mates and the building went up in flames, so while the rest of the country celebrated the liberation of Paris, I was under the knife. It was one of the worst air incidents of the war in which sixty-one people were killed; thirty-eight of them were children. I had burns to my face, hands and my right leg. Lost track of the number of operations it took for Archie to fix me, but it was between forty and fifty. That was how Bill and I met up again. I heard someone talking about how Bill Foxley's hair had grown back, so I asked where he was. We were both covered in bandages but our voices were the same.'

Ray, like Bill, has a pragmatic approach to his recovery and rehabilitation. 'You value everything more after that,' he says. 'You learn to make the most of every moment. We were lucky because of where we were. The East Grinstead people made us feel normal; they seemed to be proud of us. When we went into town we felt at home, it was our second home. It meant everything to be treated like that. To be treated as normal.'

'And we did a whole lot better with women than we did before the war,' Bill cuts in, 'we were a bit older and we were heroes. Women loved us.'

And so the conversation becomes more general and turns to memories of chasing nurses, of clandestine sex at night on the trolleys in the operating theatre; of 'knee tremblers' in the linen room, stumpy webbed fingers fumbling with fly buttons, suspenders and bras, and unscrewing the light bulbs in the hospital phone box. They talk of teasing the nurses and playing tricks on them. I ask how the nurses felt about it.

'They loved it,' someone says.

'What—all of them? No one objected?'

This incites more laughter and more memories of the young women of the Voluntary Aid Detachment (VADs) who were posted to the hospital.

'Virgins Awaiting Destruction,' someone says, 'lovely girls.'

'We wouldn't have survived without the women,' Bill Foxley says. 'They kept us alive in more than just the nursing.'

But how did *they* feel, I wonder? What did it cost them to do so much 'more than just the nursing' for this group of men who were, from all accounts, behaving like naughty schoolboys? Nursing is, at the best of times and in the best of conditions, a demanding job both physically and emotionally. In this war the home front was a different place from that which the nurses' mothers and grandmothers had known during the Great War. This time, war was on the doorstep, overhead, around every corner. You woke each day breathing danger, and fell asleep at night wondering if you would still be there in the morning. Not for nothing was it called the 'home front'. Neighbours, relatives, friends and lovers could disappear overnight, you could come home from work to find your home a pile of rubble, pop out for some milk and find the corner shop gone. How did these women turn up for work for days on end, with rarely a break, nurse their patients and deliver that extra dimension of care that gave these men the will to live with their terrible injuries?

I drive away from The Hedgehog anxious that I may have lost the knack of interviewing. Today I got what I had hoped for, a glimpse of the Guinea Pig culture. I also gathered more stories, but they, like the written memoirs, all have a sameness about them. Despite my genuine interest in the subject, and decades of experience with various types of interviews, I haven't yet succeeded in digging deeper. The men tell me their stories in such similar ways. They recount what happened: the events, the results, the injuries, the operations. There are the familiar jokes, the constant references to others who were worse off, to the surgeon who made them his own, and became their friend and mentor, and to the life-sustaining brotherhood of the Guinea Pig Club. And then there is the almost mantra-like summing up. Perhaps it is the effect of having told their stories so frequently and for so long. Perhaps it is McIndoe's prescient advice that they must stick together and support each other if they were to survive the war and the challenge of the postwar years. I've always been able to draw out meaning and encourage reflection, but with each Guinea Pig I hit a wall of narrative in which attempts to probe deeper are always sidetracked into humour.

Is this what memorialisation does? Does the constant telling of the personal and collective version of events form a crust that concretises the heroic tale and makes it bearable?

Is it a way of living with the past, of armouring the self against the agony of re-living it? And what happens if someone starts to chip away at it? This is, after all, what I am trying to do, although I'm making a poor job of it so far; chipping away at the stories, wanting more, chipping away at my own nostalgia for the past. What happens to them, to me, if it all crumbles?

7. THE GUINEA PIGS AND THEIR CLUB

It was after the end of the Great War that the Royal Air Force emerged from the control of the army and navy as an independent force, and its leaders moved to reinforce that independence with a distinctive culture of modernity. Martin Francis writes that 'Flyers saw themselves as a completely new class of warriors, men whose bravery and skill would be tested by their ability to wage war using the most advanced technology available.' The culture was one of meritocracy, based to a great extent on character although, as Francis points out, the recruiting officers of the RAF judged character '... in terms of the qualities exemplified by the private schools and elite universities they themselves had attended.'[19] Even so, the service offered opportunities for others to rise from the lower ranks and it soon became notable for its more casual approach to uniform and behaviour than the army and navy, both of which viewed the flyers with some disapproval and disdain. By the time the threat of a second war became reality, young men who were ready to enlist had grown up with heroic tales of the first flyers in the Great War, and with the exciting fictional escapades of the dashing Captain James Bigglesworth. 'Biggles' was the creation of Captain W. E. Johns, himself a World War I pilot, who wrote more than a hundred volumes including novels and short stories, about his fictional hero. The books were originally written for older adolescents but some were adjusted for younger readers. Biggles's popularity was unrivalled and while the stories always emphasised the values of honesty and bravery, the racism, sexism and indifference to violent death are frequently confronting for contemporary readers. These ripping yarns about life in the air and the heroic deeds of Biggles and his pals stood out among the comparatively dull reading material for adolescent boys between the wars.

By the late 30s a number of British universities had their own air squadrons where undergraduates could learn to fly free of charge and many were encouraged to enlist in the RAF. The image of the service was tinged with the glamour of its conquest of the air, a reputation for bravery and the most attractive uniform. The RAF also had a reputation for a rather dashing sort of slackness when it came to service discipline. There is a popular assumption that the wartime flyers and particularly the fighter pilots came largely from wealthy or aristocratic families, and had been schooled in the country's top private schools, but the records indicate that seventy per cent of pilots were state educated with the remaining thirty per cent the product of private schools. Of these, only eight per cent had been schooled in the hallowed halls of Eton, Harrow and the other elite establishments. And the men of Bomber and Fighter Commands were by no means all British; their backgrounds were diverse and included Polish, Czechoslovakian, Belgian, Canadian and Australian men who served alongside their British counterparts.

The RAF was very much a man's world with a heavy drinking culture. It frequently attracted young men who relished risk and danger and, particularly among the fighter pilots, a strong sense of individualism. 'The flyboys' as they were sometimes called, cultivated a reputation for reckless driving and heavy drinking which did not endear them to large sections of the public in the pre-war years. Parents warned their daughters of the dangers of associating with this new brand of servicemen. But the glamour of the RAF and the seemingly superhuman nature of flight were undoubtedly good for egos. It's easy to imagine the flyboys careering at speed and swerving dramatically up muddy banks to avoid collisions on these narrow, home counties roads, where even today it is not possible for two cars coming from opposite directions to pass each other. Easy to imagine them in their glamorous uniforms or leather flying jackets swinging into the car park of the local pub and making an entrance designed to attract the attention of the local women.

The fairly widespread pre-war public disapproval of the RAF hardened to hostility during the first half of 1940, despite the dogged air battles fought over France. This was fuelled to some extent by the army, which felt that the RAF had failed the British Expeditionary Force in the evacuation from Dunkirk. RAF personnel were frequently abused and sometimes assaulted by soldiers and civilians, and were frozen out of pubs where they had previously been welcomed as regulars. It was the Battle of Britain in the late summer of that year that transformed the flyers into heroes, although the change in public perception was by no means instant or universal. In their periods of leave the presence of fighter pilots in pubs and hotels, and driving recklessly around the countryside was a reality that still irked many on the home front.[20] But there was no doubt that the dashing, heroic image of flyers who returned so frequently to the air despite the devastating loss of their comrades, was irresistible to some, especially to women. The RAF suffered devastating losses in the Battle of Britain: 544 aircrew were killed, 422 wounded and 1,547 aircraft destroyed. 'Never in the field of human conflict was so much owed by so many to so few,' Churchill said in his speech of 20th August 1940.[21] While 'the few' is often assumed to refer to the men of Fighter Command he was also referring to Bomber Command. And for both, of course, there was much more to come.

The popular image of the wartime flyer has, to some extent, been informed by *The Last Enemy,* a fictional memoir written by Spitfire pilot Richard Hillary, first published in 1943. The book is generally placed at the forefront of World War II literature in a similar way to the work of the poets of the Great War: Wilfred Owen, Siegfried Sassoon and Rupert Brooke. Hillary, a Sydney-born Australian, had grown up in England attending Shrewsbury—one of the middle-range schools—and continued on to Trinity College, Oxford where he developed a reputation as an oarsman and had enrolled in the university's Air Squadron. He was outstandingly good-looking, charming, sophisticated and daring. He was also arrogant, cocky, argumentative and frequently supercilious.[22] On 3rd September 1939, Hillary, then two years into his degree, listened to Neville Chamberlain's speech with its declaration of war and promptly drove from his parents' home in Beaconsfield to the Squadron headquarters where he was put in charge of an undergraduate platoon. He was called up into the RAF in October. A year later, in the heat of the Battle of Britain, his aircraft was hit by enemy fire after a battle with a German Messerschmitt. The Spitfire burst into flames and when Hillary attempted to open the hood of the cockpit, it stuck. Precious minutes passed before he could force it partially open. By that time his mask and oxygen cylinder were on fire and he lost consciousness, regaining it only as he was spiralling towards the unwelcoming waters of the North Sea. Supported by his life jacket, and horribly aware of the smell of his own burned flesh, he floated for several hours before he was spotted and rescued by the Margate lifeboat and taken to the local hospital.

During the flight Hillary had removed his gloves and goggles, and when he caught sight of his hands in the water he saw that the skin was shredded to the bone and burned back as far as his wrists. At a second look he could see nothing and believed he had also lost his sight. When his parents arrived to visit him in hospital, his arms and legs were encased in bandages, and he hung, suspended by straps of webbing, a few inches above his hospital bed. His face and hands were covered in a black shell of tannic acid, his eyes coated with gentian violet. Five days later he was transferred to the Royal Masonic Hospital in London, where the surgeon who chipped away the tannic acid discovered septicaemia. His fingers had been drawn back into claws and were fused to his palms. It was here that Hillary came face to face with Archibald McIndoe, and was moved to East Grinstead. Richard Hillary was one of McIndoe's early surgical guinea pigs, and certainly the most difficult personality but, although destined to clash time and again, the two men eventually developed a mutual respect. The acute pain of injuries, the fear of a lost future, and the crisis of identity and masculinity created by facial disfigurement meant that all the men on Ward III were both physically and emotionally traumatised. Most relied on the camaraderie of the ward, the inspiration of the surgeon, the support of the local community and eventually the establishment of the Guinea Pig Club, to keep them from despair. But Hillary was a case apart. His courage and success in the air, his brutal cutting down and facial injuries meant that he had much in common with his fellow patients. He was a typical Guinea Pig in everything but his personal way of recovery, unpopular with both staff and patients for his rudeness, irritability, and arrogance, and although he was one of the founder members of the Guinea Pig Club his nature meant that he never embraced its spirit or ethos, a fact that may have contributed to his tragic death a couple of years later.

The Last Enemy is a distinctively personal story, in which Hillary admitted he spiced up the truth with a dash of fiction. That dash seems mainly to have been included in the service of making meaning of his experiences for both himself and his readers, and it is this that sets it aside, in literary rather than historical terms, from the other significant and more traditional Guinea Pig memoirs. There are several of these, and as a reader of most I found William Simpson's *I Burned My Fingers*, Geoffrey Page's *Shot Down in Flames,* and Tom Gleave's *I Had a Row With a German,* to be the most enlightening and insightful. What they lack in literary finesse is more than compensated for by the humanity and modesty that is lacking in Hillary's book.

*

It has been raining on and off for weeks and now solidly for several days. Vast areas of the country are under water. The news is full of stories of people being rescued from their rooftops in small boats; domestic and farm animals are drowning, sewage is seeping into the water supply and whole communities, cut off by floods, wait for fresh water supplies to be dropped to them. Aerial footage of the motorways shows lines of cars stalled in water that is creeping up to window level while the occupants are trapped inside. I stand at the window of the studio watching as the last vestiges of Malcolm's garden disappear under water, and remember the flood of 1968. I was eight-and-a-half months pregnant and terrified that I might go into labour and not be able to get to hospital through the floods. I wonder how many women are, right now, packing their overnight bags and praying for someone to come and get them and their unborn babies to safety. The local radio news reports that the London to Eastbourne railway line is underwater and East Grinstead station is closed. Eventually Malcolm appears through the rain dressed from head to foot in heavy-duty PVC like a North Sea trawler-man, trudging through the water, wielding a crowbar to open the soak wells. The lane is flooded and impassable, he tells me as water surges around us. If it stops this afternoon we may be able to get out tomorrow or the day after. If it keeps raining we're in serious trouble.

Whatever else about England may have changed in the postwar decades, the weather at least is consistent. July 1941 was, similarly, a month of exceptional rainfall, with the possibility of dangerous flooding in some regional areas. The morning of Sunday 20th dawned with torrential rain that filled the grounds of the Queen Victoria Hospital with massive puddles and flooded the pathways. Nurses wrapped their capes around them and scuttled, heads down, between the buildings. Very early that morning, from the window of Ward III, Roger* recalls watching as two nurses lost their starched white caps to the fierce, rain-soaked wind.

'I remember that morning very clearly,' he says. 'It was foul, just like my mood. I had a monstrous hangover. I took a look at the weather, and went back to bed. A few of us had really overdone it the night before. So I had several hours more kip and that's why I wasn't there at the beginning of the club. I've always regretted that—not being there at the start.'

The ward was quiet that morning, the silence broken only by snores as some of the more rowdy inhabitants slept off the effects of the previous night. Unlike the light and airy wards in the main hospital building, the burns unit in its army hut frequently felt confined and airless. Despite McIndoe's attempts to make it more homely and hospitable it was an inadequate and overcrowded space full of disfigured and disabled men, where the smell of alcohol, sweat and wounded bodies competed with the acrid fumes of Lysol disinfectant and salt water. The scent of the fresh flowers that McIndoe insisted upon did little to moderate this. The staff were doubtless thankful for a little respite; the work on Ward III was intense and never-ending. Nurses and orderlies spent long days on their feet dressing wounds, getting patients into and out of the saline baths, dispensing medication, feeding and washing patients, preparing them for surgery and welcoming them back, delivering bedpans and managing the high spirits and pranks of the patients along with all their other work. Thanks to a surfeit of alcohol the night before there was a modicum of peace that morning as the few patients who surfaced got dressed or shambled off in their dressing-gowns, through the rain, to a nearby hut that was used as an entertainment area. They were in search of some hair of the dog, while the rest lay snoring until long past normal waking time.[23]

As the rain pounded on the roof of the entertainment hut one of the men who had usable hands opened a bottle of sherry and the mood began to lift. By mid-morning, when the rain gave way to watery sunshine, something significant had happened. The assembled company had agreed to form a 'grogging club'. Among those present that morning were Pilot Officer Geoffrey Page, Squadron Leader Tom Gleave, a Czech fighter pilot, Frankie Truhlar, Richard Hillary and Wing Commander Derek Martin. They named themselves The Maxillonian Club, after the maxillo-facial surgery they had all undergone. With their characteristic dark and often ironic humour the men elected Flying Officer Bill Towers-Perkins as secretary because his badly burned fingers meant he was unable to write letters. The treasurer was Pilot Officer Peter Weeks whose legs were so severely burned that he was confined to a wheelchair and could not abscond with the funds. Tom Gleave was appointed Vice President and, later that day, McIndoe was persuaded to become President. It was a few months later that the name was changed to the Guinea Pig Club. The requirement for membership was that a man must be a member of the RAF, 'mashed, fried or boiled' in the service, and treated at East Grinstead. McIndoe's staff were also made members and included assistant surgeon Percy Jayes and anaesthetist John Hunter. Some time later, Group Captain Ross Tilley of the Royal Canadian Air Force. Many of RCAF aircrew were being treated at East Grinstead and Tilley, who had a background in plastic surgery, had been sent by the Canadian Government to work with McIndoe. The two discovered an instant rapport, which developed into a powerful and lasting working relationship and close friendship. Another important member of the club was Flight Sergeant Edward Blacksell, a former schoolteacher who had hoped to join the navy, but was turned down so applied to the RAF where he was sent to the School for Physical Training Instructors. After a short spell with the Australian contingent in RAAF No. 10 Squadron in Plymouth, Blacksell was ordered to report to McIndoe at East Grinstead where he was appointed as Welfare Officer with the task of caring for the welfare and fitness of the RAF patients. Unsurprisingly, in view of the times, the women, even the senior nurses such as Jill Mullins, were excluded from the club.

It was Geoffrey Page who eventually came up with the idea that the club could be more than just an excuse for excessive alcohol consumption. Page, who had little faith in the idea that disability pensions would be made available after the war, suggested that those men who were able to return either to active service or normal civilian life might do something to ensure that the less fortunate members could be looked after financially.[24] It all took time, but McIndoe was quick to see the potential of the club as a vital part of his therapeutic treatment model. It brought the men together with a sense of purpose, camaraderie and commitment, and it could keep them together over the coming years when so many would need to return time and again for further operations. The appointment of Blacksell as Welfare Officer had proved a huge advantage; he was a strong, genial and reassuring presence, and the respect and affection he inspired in the patients ensured that he also frequently acted as counsellor and peacekeeper as well as managing the accounts and membership records and much more. Eventually the club members, led by McIndoe, were able to secure the support of the RAF Benevolent Society. A fund was established and by 1943, when Richard Hillary's book *The Last Enemy* was released and began to attract considerable attention, donations began to flow in to the club's coffers.

Annual reunions ensured that those who had moved on remained linked to the club and in his various tussles with the RAF and the Ministry of Health, McIndoe had the reputation and strength of the club behind him. Emily Mayhew points out that the members of the Guinea Pig Club became famous throughout the country '... the first and only time in modern British history that a large group of casualties achieved a sustained level of public interest and acclaim.'[25] Those Sunday morning hangovers had been the start of an extraordinary organisation that helped to save the lives, the sanity, and the emotional stability of men whose lives had been changed by fire, and to support their income and their widows. It seems unlikely that on that first wet and windy morning, or during the early months and years of the club's life, any of its members would have dreamed they would be returning to East Grinstead for reunions into the first decade of a new century.

8. ON FEAR AND SILENCE

Still cut off by the flooded lane and confined to the studio, I develop an unhealthy relationship with the most mundane British reality TV, home renovations and auctions, crime watching, and food programs. Particularly nauseating is *Come Dine With Me,* in which six contestants (all strangers) each take turns to hold a dinner party in their home for the others. Their awkwardness around the table, the tension of passive aggression, the lack of insight on the part of the participants into what is actually happening, epitomises what I think is the worst of the genre. As each participant is interviewed on their way home and must critique the food, the host, the hospitality, the home and the success or otherwise of the evening, the arrogant and vicious backstabbing is breathtaking. It's so awful that I rapidly become addicted to it and find myself, alone in the studio, raging at the contestants. Perhaps it is because I am still trapped in the search for the England of my childhood and youth, reading and trying to write about a way of being that has a special place in my memory. In Australia I could watch this program with disgust but it would elicit just a shrug of the shoulders as a sign of the times, rather than outrage at what seems like an assault on my nostalgic image of England. It's ridiculous and self-indulgent. Does it perhaps insult my memory?

I had a privileged childhood, the only child of conservative, middle-class parents, at a time when seediness and bad behaviour were supposed to be hidden from public view. Never mind what went on in the deprived corners of northern industrial towns, the poverty-stricken slums of London, the vicious crime-ridden streets of Soho, or the corrupt enclaves of high society, my little niche of England was coated with a patina of respectability and modesty which I took for granted. In actuality, the darker side was always close at hand. The English are, after all, world champions in the art of passive aggression; the backstabbing among the aristocracy is equalled only by that which goes on over the garden fence and in the pub. Even in the peaceful Sussex countryside of the 1940s and 50s, racial prejudice and homophobia were rife, and a woman's place was most definitely in the home irrespective of what role she may have excelled in during the war.

But memories of my idyllic childhood are all around me: picking primroses with my mother in sunlit country lanes, hiding with my friend Evelyn inside the huge rhododendron bush in the garden, learning to ride a pony, ballet classes, sipping a daring Babycham with my prawn cocktail, my first long dress. We make of it what we will, what we wish for, and what we need to believe, and create meaning through the act of remembering. But how accurate is it? And is what we remember necessarily more important than what we have forgotten? Have I allowed my version of the past to settle into permanence, to become something I want to change or challenge? Did I honestly believe I could find the England I had left behind intact, that I could recapture that past simply by being here?

The rain has stopped but the flooded lane is still impassable and I have to abandon my plans to set off to Oxford. It's hugely disappointing as I have finally located one of McIndoe's nurses who is willing to talk to me. Lady Moira Nelson is the widow of Sir Frank Nelson who headed the Special Operations Executive during the war, and we have already had some brief correspondence. I have high hopes of getting a woman's view of life in Ward III, and the impact of boyish high jinks on the nursing staff. I call with apologies, praying she won't take this postponement as a reason to pull out, but much of Oxford is also underwater and she tells me that next week will, hopefully, be fine. We do all the appropriate jokes about the English weather and she sounds cheerful and robust.

'I'll see you next week and we'll have a nice afternoon tea together. And I've got some phone numbers for you—other nurses.'

I've been running out of options for tracing nurses. The contacts I had acquired from various sources have fizzled out in unanswered emails, disconnected telephone numbers and letters returned with 'deceased' or 'not at this address' scrawled across them. I've even taken to accosting elderly people in the street and asking them if they were here during the war. The responses have been amused and friendly but so far yielded nothing, so Moira Nelson and her phone numbers seem to herald a breakthrough.

Meanwhile I am stuck indoors, trawling the internet for material on how men, and particularly RAF aircrew, coped with fear. Jack Toper and all the other Guinea Pigs I have met have avoided the issue of fear, and this also seems to be the case in recorded interviews I have watched and read. 'If I could go back,' they say, 'I wouldn't change it. I would rather have gone through this than not be a Guinea Pig.' The words may vary but the meaning does not change. Alongside it is the disavowal of fear—'I didn't feel any fear when I was on a mission.' The Guinea Pigs themselves speak as though fear came only later, at a time when, confined to a hospital bed, they contemplated a future truncated by terrible disfigurement, disablement, and what seemed then to be a certainty that they had been rendered unlovable.

So, is their matter-of-fact telling of their combat experiences a learned behaviour—a mask that helped them to preserve their sense of masculinity at a time when understandings of manliness did not allow for the admission of fear? Did the thrill of flying—the adrenaline it released—temporarily anaesthetise fear to the extent that they could perform as warriors? Could it have worked at a deeper level that allowed them to subdue a terrible fear within themselves? And what right do I have to probe this with men who have learned to live with those memories?

Joanna Bourke, who has written widely on the male psyche in both world wars, and on the topic of fear itself, writes that fear was the most dominant of emotions in combat and was the soldier's persistent adversary irrespective of rank.[26] And war historian Paul Fussell suggests that in World War II heavy drinking was the answer to fear, boredom and the terrible damage to the sense of identity experienced by so many combatants. Drunkenness, he writes, did for the men of this war what drugs did for the next generation in Vietnam.[27]

Those of us who have not lived through war, not had to risk our lives in the service of our country nor had to endure experiences and injuries that have the potential to destroy our sense of ourselves, can only begin to imagine what that means. The urge to attribute one's own meaning and interpretation is a hazard, and writing about war is frequently conflicted. Fear is an intrinsic part of war, and the manifestations of anxiety, vulnerability and despair that are its demons must be profoundly intimate and sometimes also collective.

The RAF was well aware of the dimensions of fear and the threat it presented to discipline, morale and the performance of its aircrew. Overcoming, or at least managing, both the collective and individual fear of its flyers was a priority. Courage was expected – it was, after all, an essential ingredient of normative masculinity of the time, and the RAF attracted young men whose off-duty behaviour demonstrated that they wanted to live life to the full. The behaviour of the flyboys that so offended the residents of the small towns and villages of England speaks of a lust for life, and a need to live for the moment without thinking too much about what tomorrow might bring.

There were a variety of horrifying ways in which flyers could visualise death, injury, and disablement. To be consumed fully or partially by fire was an obvious threat, as was the risk of being sucked out of a pressurised compartment, being hit by flying debris, being shot down and drowning at sea or crashing on land, and then being captured by the enemy. None of these or other scenarios were purely imaginary. Every day there were stories of death and disaster, the loss of limbs, faces and heads being blown away, and men enveloped by fire. Friends and comrades routinely climbed into their aircraft never to be seen again, or to return with horrific and disabling injuries. In addition to the risks of combat, flying training also resulted in devastating injuries and loss of life. Despite this, there is no doubt that, for many, an equally paralysing fear was that of being thought a coward.[28]

'I can't make sense of it,' I say much later to a friend, an Australian Vietnam veteran, now in his late sixties and living in London. We have known each other for years but he never talks about his own experience of combat. 'These men talked to me about what happened, they relate quite a lot of detail, usually in a very lighthearted way, they talk about their injuries, and their struggle to face the world, but never about fear, never about how it felt and what really went on in their heads.'

'Good lord, you want blood don't you?' he says. 'Of course they don't talk about that. It's not something you can talk about; it would destroy you. You get to be with other men who've been through it and don't have to talk about it because you all know. It doesn't have to be spoken. You can't talk to people who weren't there. Impossible. Look, in a war you see things no one should ever see and sometimes you have to do things that no one should have to do. Some people find how to talk about what happened, but you're not going to get them to tell you how it felt, what you went through, not how it was to live through it. That's like a monster and you're always trying to keep it at bay. You're certainly not going to have a friendly chat about it to some nosey writer who turns up on your doorstep.'

He goes on to talk about post-traumatic stress disorder (PTSD) in a general way and then in relation to World War II veterans. 'It was different for them than for us,' he says. 'Worse probably, because the diagnosis didn't come until more than thirty years after their war was over. There was no way for them to deal with it. Having a diagnosis made it real for other people, who hadn't been through it, to understand. Before that ... well you'd have no way of talking, except I suppose you might joke about it. You'd worry about sounding like a coward. Trust me,' he says as he heads off home, 'there are limits to what you can expect. Some things you're just going to have to let go.'

Perhaps it is the fluency, simplicity and self-deprecating humour with which the Guinea Pigs tell their stories that has led me to expect more, and to assume that everything is now neatly filed away in their memories, ready to discuss with anyone who asks. Traumatic memories haunt the subconscious and can rise to the surface at any time, irrespective of the passing of time, and create chaos. Reassembling and organising those memories can defy language and attempting to do so can be disabling. I can see now how that the fraternity of the club, built on the knowledge of traumatic experience that does not have to be articulated, can create a bond that makes it possible to live with that experience. I am shocked and ashamed that it has taken this long for me to translate what I know theoretically about post-traumatic memory into this context.

War writer and journalist Sebastian Junger describes in a TED Talk his experience in combat with American soldiers in Afghanistan. Junger articulates understandings that also seem relevant to the desire to return to service as soon as possible—something all the Guinea Pigs mention. And it is as much about brotherhood as it is about the restoration of self-esteem and identity.

'Any sane person hates war, hates the idea of war, wouldn't want to have anything to do with it, doesn't want to be near it, doesn't want to know about it,' Junger says. He goes on to point out that even so, most of us would pay money to go to the cinema to watch a war movie. 'And trust me,' he continues, 'if a room full of peace-loving people finds something compelling about war, so do twenty-year old soldiers who have been trained in it.'

To understand this, Junger explains, you have to think about combat neurologically and not in a moral sense. 'Let's think about what happens in your brain when you're in combat. First of all the experience is a very bizarre one. It's not what I had expected. Usually, you are not scared. [...] Time slows down. You get this weird tunnel vision. You notice some details very, very, very, accurately and other things drop out. It's almost a slightly altered state of mind.' This is the effect, he explains, of massive amounts of adrenaline pumping through the system. 'Young men will go to great lengths to have that experience. It's wired into us. It's hormonally supported. The mortality rate for young men in society is six times that of young women from violence and from accidents, just the stupid stuff that young men do; jumping off things ... lighting fires ...'

Junger goes on to talk about the determination to return to battle; he talks about brotherhood—something he describes as 'in some way the opposite of killing'. This, he suggests, is why men want and need to go back. Brotherhood, he says, is different from friendship. 'Brotherhood has nothing to do with how you feel about the other person. It's a mutual agreement in a group that you will put the welfare of the group, you will put the safety of everyone in the group, above your own. In effect you are saying, I love these other people more than I love myself.'[29]

I think of the stories of flyers like Bill Foxley and others, who escaped without injury from burning wreckage only to turn back to the furnace to rescue a colleague, and of the men who pleaded with McIndoe to sign them off as fit for a return to combat, and fought their superior officers to be allowed back into action. It all makes sense as Junger speaks of soldiers having a bond in which they loved the others more than they loved themselves, and how it feels to find yourself cut adrift from that. 'You think about how good that would feel,' he asks his audience, 'imagine it, and they are blessed with that experience. When they come home and are just back in society like the rest of us are, not knowing who they can count on, not knowing who loves them, who they can love, not knowing exactly what anyone they know would do for them if it came down to it. That is terrifying. Compared to that, war, psychologically, in some ways, is easy, compared to that kind of alienation.'[30]

The Guinea Pigs' 'grogging club' provided a brotherhood of combat that could be sustained over the years. Drinking with a purpose among comrades was, and still is, a common and powerful ritual of masculinity. It was certainly a wartime survival mechanism in all the services and in much of civilian life. Martin Francis suggests that for aircrew there was the added dimension of total reliance on the most recent technological advances in the hardware of war, an image of modernity and sophistication in that vast and infinitely unknowable world of the air.[31] For the lone fighter pilot, fear could all too easily invade and occupy the cockpit. Its haunting presence had to be subdued before it could take control. Fighter pilots were, by and large, of a type that needed personal control over their own circumstances. Trusting their fate to others was not to their liking, and self-reliance was a feature of the fighter's character. As Richard Hillary writes:

> The flyer is of a race of men who since time immemorial have been inarticulate; who, through their daily contact with death, have realized, often enough unconsciously, certain fundamental things. It is only in the air that the pilot can grasp that feeling, that flash of knowledge, of insight, that matures him beyond his years; only in the air that he knows suddenly he is a man in a world of men. 'Coming back to earth' has for him a double significance. He finds it difficult to orientate himself in a world that is so worldly, amongst people whose conversations seems to him brilliant, minds agile, and knowledge complete—yet a people somehow blind. [...] He wants only to get back to the Mess, to be among his own kind, with men who act and don't talk, or if they do talk only shop [...] He wants to get back to that closed language that is Air Force slang.[32]

After being allowed back into active service but unable to fly solo, Richard Hillary found that having to accommodate other crew members, and to be responsible for and/or dependent on them, brought a new dimension of fear and frustration to flying. As a lone fighter pilot, he had relished the sense of agency that came with being able to fight an enemy he could see. Bomber crew on the other hand were unable to see the enemy, as poet James Dickey writes in 'The Firebombing':

> Something strange-scented falls—when those on earth/ Die, there is not even sound;/ One is cool and enthralled in the cockpit,/ [...] Deep in aesthetic contemplation,/ [...] It is this detachment,/ The honoured aesthetic evil,/ The greatest sense of power in one's life,/ That must be shed in bars, or by whatever/ Means.[33]

Bomber crews were acutely aware of the interdependence of the team and while this was a source of support, it also limited personal control. This, and the inability to see neither the enemy nor the extent of the destruction their mission created, had its own neuroses and was, for some, an added pressure. It is easy to imagine that whatever the hardware, however strongly the adrenaline surged, the effort to perform as expected in close proximity to others who rely on you, was certain to take its toll.

For the men of the RAF, suppression of fear carved itself into minds and bodies and manifested in blinding headaches, nightmares, insomnia, digestive problems, shaking limbs, the inability to concentrate, delusions in which flyers saw their own death, and the beginnings of mental breakdown.[34] The punishing rounds of sorties were spaced out with intervals of downtime, but they were short intervals; enough to provide a chance to rest but not long enough to allow for a sense of disconnection that might allow a man to relax his grip and never get it back again. The constant and intense pressure and pace of life as a flyer became so much a way of life that in those intervals rest was replaced with other forms of action and intensity. The lust for life was channelled into heavy drinking, wild parties, fast and risky driving, and whenever possible, sex, sex, sex. Finding a manageable way to tell the story would have been—still is—something to hang on to, a recipe for normalcy and a tool to recover and live with an unbearable past.

9. LIFE ON WARD III

Since my first visit to the hospital with Bob Marchant I've returned several times to search the archives of the Guinea Pig Museum, and on each occasion I have taken time to sit alone in the café in an effort to conjure up the atmosphere of Ward III but without much success. The rattle of crockery and cutlery, the hum of conversation, the scrape of chair legs, a child having a tantrum, and the noises from the kitchen are tremendously distracting although they may well be similar to the level of noise that was not uncommon during the Guinea Pig days. Similar, in fact, to what Flight Engineer Alan Morgan heard when he arrived on Ward III, suffering from pneumonia and confused with shock. Alan had been an apprentice toolmaker in Stockport at the start of the war, and had wanted to join the navy but had been turned down. He was in a reserved occupation, needed in the factory, forced to content himself with being indispensable.

'I had no idea where I was. It sounded like a nuthouse. I thought they were all a load of nutters. I just kept thinking—this is a bloody place and they're all bloody mad in here.'

Alan wasn't just thinking it, he was saying it too—frequently and loudly—to anyone who would listen. What he heard was not the sort of noise normally associated with a hospital ward but loud voices, raucous laughter, swearing, the clink of glasses, the radio that was switched on all day, the sound of beds being moved, tuneless singing, dance music from the gramophone, even a bicycle bell, as well as the softer voices and laughter of women. At night he heard men returning from the local pub somewhat the worse for wear, and nurses trying to hush them. It was the sound of people having a good time; a sound that frequently drowned out the harsh cries and gut-wrenching moans of acute pain, but was also punctuated with sudden outbursts of anger or despair. All life was there in that ward, unlike the hushed, muted atmosphere he expected. The ward was as close to home—as close to normal life—as McIndoe could make it and of course it had the added benefits of beautiful nurses, and brothers in arms. It was a place where, as I was beginning to understand, social mores counted for little and boundaries were breached as a matter of course, and frequently on the orders of the surgeon.

For a man whom many outsiders saw as unsympathetic and detached, McIndoe demonstrated an extraordinary empathy with his 'boys'. He treated them with respect, looking dispassionately at their injuries and never shielding them from unpalatable truths. To reduce their fear he encouraged them to sit in the gallery and watch him operate. The accommodation at East Grinstead was limited and as patient numbers mounted he made a virtue of necessity by dispensing with the traditional segregation of officers and ranks.

'It were amazing to me to see that the person in the next bed were an officer, and that everyone mucked in together,' Alan Morgan told me. 'Rank meant nothing; we were all the same. That was Archie's rule and no one ever argued with it. If the officer in the next bed were in better shape than you he'd bring you a cuppa, put the sugar in, stir it and hold it for you to drink. It took me a time to get used to that I can tell you.'

Ward III came as a surprise to patients, visitors, and to the hospital's Welfare Committee. The radio and gramophone, the sight of a heavily bandaged patient or one with a pedicle connecting his face to his arm or chest, attempting to persuade a busy nurse to dance with him, the permanent fixture of a barrel with an endless supply of (slightly watered down) beer to keep the men's spirits up, were unlike anything seen in the hospital before the war. Ribald jokes and abuse flew back and forth between the beds, and somewhere in that ward you could be sure a patient was doing his best to chat up a nurse.

In 1940 McIndoe had won a significant battle with the Hospital Welfare Committee whose members had complained about the bad language, noise, rudeness, drinking and flirting. The members made regular rounds of the wards and were accustomed to grateful, respectful and compliant patients; the behaviour of patients on Ward III shocked and offended them. Frustrated by what he saw as their narrow-mindedness and lack of understanding, McIndoe confronted the committee head-on at a meeting. The hospital, he told them, was no longer solely for the local community, but was primarily for the physical and mental rebuilding of injured airmen and their specific problems. While many had horrific injuries and needed multiple operations, they were not actually sick, but their injuries were devastating and had the potential to destroy their spirits. It was his job, he said, to rebuild their individual and collective morale and get them back to work. McIndoe had already won a much tougher battle for his patients' self-esteem by getting the RAF to declare them still on active duty. This allowed them to dispense with the regulation 'convalescent blues'—ugly, battledress style outfits made of bright blue calico that bore a strong resemblance to prison uniforms. The 'blues' had been introduced during World War I to promote a comradeship of healing among men, but while a few had enjoyed the praise and respect derived from wearing them, many more were troubled by being marked out as invalids, or convalescents. For McIndoe's boys, the blues were just another threat to their masculinity, which was already under siege, and this victory meant they could continue wear their uniforms when they went into the town, home to convalesce or out on excursions to London or the coast which McIndoe organised. It was a vital move in restoring self-respect. Roger, an officer Guinea Pig, described to me the relief he felt on hearing that he would be allowed to wear his uniform.

'At the time it seemed like the last vestiges of self-esteem, because it was a way of thinking of myself that I tried to hang on to. To go out into the local town in uniform made me feel worthwhile, that despite my hideous face and hands I was still part of the RAF and that I had a future in the service. I don't think I could have stepped outside the hospital grounds in those ridiculous blues.'

McIndoe's strategy for recovery and reconstruction included minds as well as bodies, and it extended far beyond the confines of the hospital. He was determined to protect his patients from the reaction of a local community suddenly faced with horrifically disfigured men greeting them daily on the streets. He had closed his speech to the Welfare Committee by asking the members to use their influence in the town and to encourage local people to make his boys feel comfortable and at home. 'I don't want people going around feeling sorry for them. I don't want sympathy. I want everyone—shopkeepers, publicans, customers at the four-ale bar—to be normal with them and casual, not gape at them as if they've come out of a freak museum.'[35] The committee members were both chastened and moved and word had soon travelled around the town, but McIndoe did not leave it there. He personally set out to visit local tradespeople, publicans and community groups, and address public meetings. These men, he told the residents, had given their lives for their country, and they deserved appreciation and respect.

Margaret Streatham, now in her late eighties, and a former long-term resident of East Grinstead, remembers attending a meeting in a church hall with her mother, which she thinks was late in 1941.

'He was a very upstanding gentleman, distinguished. I remember thinking you wouldn't want to argue with him. You'd think—well I'd trust a man like that. Something he said like—well they'd risked their lives and gone through hellfire to protect you and your children—that's what he said. I'm sure those were his very words, I never forgot them. It stuck with me, you see. We were all for doing something for the war and him making it so personal you said to yourself—well I'm ready, tell me what to do.'

Margaret, who had a baby and a toddler, immediately volunteered and became a regular visitor at the hospital, reading to men who had lost or damaged sight, and writing letters for them. Sam, Margaret's husband, was in the army and she and the children were living with her mother.

'Then we heard that people sometimes needed somewhere to stay. Some of the lads had mothers or wives, ordinary people like us, hard up you know, couldn't afford much. So we'd put them up for a night or two. Mum had a third bedroom, I had the kids in with me and we give the other room for the visitors. It doesn't seem much now but we wanted to do our bit. I think it helped them to have someone to talk to when they came back from the hospital. It was a terrible shock for them seeing their sons and hubbies like that. Some of the ladies left straight away and I'm told they didn't come back. Couldn't face it you see. Very sad that.'

Getting women into the wards as volunteers, and as companions for the convalescent aircrew was important to McIndoe who believed that the presence of beautiful women was crucial to recovery and the restoration of the men's self-esteem. It is widely recorded that he chose his nurses first for their professional excellence and—a very close second—for their looks. There were no plain or unattractive women among his nursing staff, and even this was not enough—they also had to have a sense of humour. Some weeks later in my stay, McIndoe's younger daughter, Vanora Marland, confirmed this and spoke further about her late father's attitude to women.

'My father wanted the best nurses and he wanted them to be beautiful and they had to be the sort of women who wouldn't make a fuss about having their bottoms pinched. The men were young and some had girlfriends who couldn't face their terrible injuries and had deserted them. He thought having beautiful women around to flirt with was good for them and he encouraged it. They had been handsome, dashing young men and if anything was going to restore their self-esteem it was the presence of beautiful women who were interested in them.' He was, Vanora told me, very much a man of his time. 'He loved women, loved to be surrounded by them, but at the same time he didn't think much of them aside from their use to men. He thought they should just be there for men. He loved those boys and would do anything for them and he looked for nurses, and local women for parties or dancing or helping in the hospital—the sort of girls who wouldn't make a fuss and who'd flirt and take a joke.'

Once again I can't help wondering how amusing it was to some of the nurses to be the receiving end of the pinches and the jokes. What did it cost them in the suppression of feeling, to play along with a boisterous crowd of young men who were frequently out of control?

Still confined by the weather, I search the internet for stories of nurses from Ward III that will throw any light on the nurses' experience but with no success. But much later, in the BBC Archive, *The People's War*, I discover a series of contributions by Margaret Chadd who was the almoner at East Grinstead during the war years. In 1945 Chadd gave a presentation on her role at London University, in which she described the East Grinstead policy under McIndoe as comprising the 'three Rs of hospital treatment, namely Responsibility, Rehabilitation and Resettlement.' And she explains the complex work of the rehabilitation of long-term patients, which cannot be undertaken within the normal routine of the hospital:

> The patient is encouraged to feel that he belongs to the hospital and must behave himself accordingly, rather to a code of honour than by a set of rigid rules. He is then made to feel an important person in his own right within the hospital and bears the responsibility for its well-being. Any rules that exist are surgical rather than social.[36]

This philosophical position established by McIndoe conjures up an ideal model of mutual responsibility and patient conduct that was far simpler in its intent than in its execution. The policy, for all its good intentions, was interpreted in ways that could have a dramatic impact on nurses and the conduct of nursing. Forty years later, in a presentation made to the Norfolk and General Hospital in 1987, Margaret Chadd described a culture that was in direct contravention of the theoretical code of honour she had outlined in her earlier presentation:

> The nursing staff was under the jurisdiction of Matron Hall, a warm, loveable and approachable Irish lady of middle age who tried so hard to keep a firm hand on the 'lads'. This often proved difficult as the hospital was not like a normal cottage hospital once the service personnel arrived. She often had great difficulty in keeping control when they got up to their pranks; more often than not in high spirits having been down to the local pub in the evening. If she made any comment to McIndoe, his reply would be, 'These men have had to put up with a hell of a lot, so surely you and your staff can put up with a little bit of nonsense.' It depended on how you interpreted 'little' and "nonsense'. If you saw one of the ward sisters, loudly shrieking and being carried in the arms of a pyjama clad patient towards a cold bath would you intervene or punish? What could you say to patients returning late at night, after a visit to the local pub, having collected up all the roadwork lanterns and on returning to their ward singing, cheering, waving the lanterns up and down and waking everyone who was asleep?[37]

Bearing in mind the youth of so many of the patients, their horrifying injuries, and the culture of the RAF, it is easy to see how McIndoe's approach enabled them to feel as though they were living some semblance of 'normal' life and how that could help to restore their sense of identity and masculinity. Going out on the town, carousing, swearing, telling stories, drinking, occasionally fighting and being surrounded by attractive women with whom they could flirt, made them feel like men again. But some tales of the pranks on Ward III do seem to stretch the policy of mutual responsibility to an unreasonable extent. With so many patients heavily bandaged it was not uncommon for the more able patients to tease the nurses by shifting the positions of the beds when the staff were not looking, so a patient who had been on one side of the ward far from the saline bath in the morning, might be found a couple of hours later at the other end and on the other side. Some of the patients had access to bikes that they would ride up and down the wards, sometimes attaching them to a patient's bed and towing it along behind them. And those who were bed bound would often find themselves being pushed out of the hospital and up the hill into town by a group of ward mates, who would park the bed outside the Rose and Crown, and sit on it while someone went inside to get the drinks.

Anaesthetist John Hunter was very popular among the men. His large body was complemented by an expansive personality and robust sense of humour, all of which combined to put patients at ease as they were prepared for surgery. 'Just a little prick!' he would say, wielding his pre-anaesthetic needle. And he made a standing promise that if his anaesthetic made any man vomit as he came round after surgery he would buy him a drink. So as men emerged into consciousness they would find a cluster of patients sitting on the end of bed making bets on whether or not he would vomit.[38] For many of the men this environment of high-spirited fun, the teasing and practical jokes on nurses was life saving. Morale was as high as it was possible for it to be after what they had experienced.

The boundaries of acceptable and non-acceptable behaviour were always defined by what the surgeon thought 'his boys' needed for their recovery, rather than what might be fair to all parties. Both McIndoe's biographers note that his staff were expected to cope with extraordinarily difficult and challenging medical and surgical situations, together with the personal challenges created by the surgeon's expectations and his patients' behaviour. According to Mosley, nurses were told that they must radiate enthusiasm for their work 'by your efficiency, by your anxiety for the patients' welfare above all else and by your devotion to duty tempered by optimism, tact, understanding and good humour.'[39] But it seems that there were times when the line between acceptable and unacceptable behaviour had been crossed. On these occasions Matron Hall would approach McIndoe asking him to intervene or reprimand. However, while the surgeon seems to have been quick to respond to or intervene in situations outside the hospital, and particularly to those that involved any sort of damage to property, he showed little understanding or tolerance towards the women who worked for him when it came to his patients' behaviour. There are many anecdotes, like those of Margaret Chadd, that describe his blunt and dismissive manner with Matron Hall on these occasions. McIndoe's nurses were expected to provide levels of personal care and attention beyond the usual requirements of their profession. Some of the senior members of the nursing staff were sufficiently experienced and mature to manage their own situations with patients, but at the same time some had husbands or fiancés who were on active duty and who could have struggled with the ambiguity of the situation. Many of the nursing staff were young, inexperienced VADs who had received only rudimentary training from Red Cross volunteers, and had never worked anywhere, let alone a hospital men's ward, before the war catapulted them into East Grinstead. McIndoe encouraged flirting between patients and nurses, and fostered signs of relationships that might emerge from this. He encouraged the men to go out on dates with nurses, and facilitated outings, dances, theatre trips and other excursions that provided opportunities for them to socialise.

On my trawl through documents in the Imperial War Museum I had discovered the memoir of Miss Morris—a nurse at the nearby Kent and Sussex hospital in Tunbridge Wells, who had nursed several burned airmen before they were transferred to East Grinstead. She had also nursed a member of the Free French Army with whom she had developed an affinity. Some time after his discharge the former patient contacted Miss Morris and invited her out to dinner. It seems that the matron got to hear of this and Miss Morris was severely reprimanded and threatened with the sack. When she attempted to point out that the man had been discharged some weeks earlier, the matron pushed her through an open window in the nurses home. Miss Morris did stay on at the hospital but this incident provides a reminder of the behavioural standards expected of nurses at the time, and the contrast in the expectations of nurses on Ward III.[40]

On Ward III, patients found the support they needed to face their injuries. They rallied and taunted, they encouraged and commiserated, and they found ways to survive their terrible injuries and reduced abilities. The care and companionship, the generosity and the kindness of women as well as their professionalism in nursing, helped them to restore their sense of manhood, to understand that despite their disfigurement they had the chance of living a normal life, of being loved. The men came to rely on their surgeon for the truth, the possibilities, and the limitations with which they would have to face the world. It was a relationship which McIndoe described as 'closer than that which ordinarily exists between doctor and patient. The relationship begins with a clear understanding between the two of what is to take place over the years of reconstruction.'[41] Those relationships would be preserved at all costs, and any staff member who couldn't handle the pressure could find a job elsewhere. The spirit that McIndoe fostered on Ward III was a crucial part of his patients' emotional and physical survival. That spirit was an elixir of life that bound them together not only during wild nights on the town or at the pub, but through multiple operations, the agony of changing dressings, the fear of their individual futures and for some the rejection by wives and girlfriends unable to come to terms with disfigurement or disablement. A man went into surgery not only accompanied by the orderly who was pushing his trolley, but always with a Guinea Pig, or sometimes two, alongside him, holding his hand.

10. CULTURE CRISIS

Moira Nelson is waiting for me just inside the glass doors of the retirement complex. I had anticipated one of those glorious old English houses standing in its own grounds, tastefully adapted and run by charming and discreet staff as a collective home-from-home for the elderly: chandeliers, large fireplaces, floral chintz, pale carpets, and bay windows. I have clearly been watching too many BBC television dramas—both *Morse* and *Midsomer Murders* are played out in or around Oxford and the towns and villages of Oxfordshire. But instead of a grand old home with sweeping lawns, the small inner-city complex is a modest two-storey block of retirement apartments in a narrow street off the Woodstock Road, not far from the old Radcliffe Hospital; an area where one might well expect to see Morse's red Jaguar gliding by, and hear the unmistakable voice of Maria Callas floating out of the driver's window above the traffic.

Moira is leaning on her stick. She presses a buzzer to open the glass doors for me. I apologise for being late due to the impossibility of parking. 'It's quite all right, I thought I'd wait down here to let you in,' she says. 'I brought my book to keep me occupied.' She waves a paperback with a German title. 'Orwell, *Down and Out in Paris and London*. I've read it before of course but I'm re-reading this in translation—I need to keep my German brushed up.' She frequently re-reads classics in German or French, she tells me. 'You never know when you might need to use the language, it doesn't do to let things slip.' Moira is now in her late eighties, possibly more, and as we take the lift to her apartment on the second floor she talks about the importance of keeping active in body as well as mind. 'Especially when you're a woman and old,' she says. 'You know how easy it is to get pushed around. I find it helps to be on the big side too, don't you?' She is of average height and medium to plump build, with greying hair and a confident air of friendly authority.

'Make yourself comfortable,' she says once we're inside the small flat. Outside, the rain has stopped and watery sunshine floods the room with light. The table is set for tea, tiny sandwiches, mini-scones and little cakes. 'I do love afternoon tea, don't you?' Moira says.

I feel I have stepped back in time to the England of my childhood, to making the best of things, keeping oneself to oneself, to the simple pleasures of a nice afternoon tea, and the importance of putting the milk in a jug, the butter in a dish, and providing spotless linen napkins edged with cutwork. And I'm overwhelmed suddenly with sentimental nostalgia for my mother and grandmother whom I'm convinced are sighing with relief that I am keeping such admirable company. Neither would have approved of my drinking at the Hedgehog with a crowd of ageing airmen.

Moira Nelson—or Moira Carling as she was then—began her nursing training in Harrogate just before the war.

'Nursing was supposed to be a suitable occupation for nice girls, but never have nice girls been treated so badly,' she says. 'We were pitchforked into action; there were no orderlies in those days, no domestic staff and the discipline was very strict. We were on our feet from dawn to dusk—twelve-hour shifts from eight in the morning 'til eight in the evening, and then the night shifts were twelve hours too. We prepared the porridge for breakfast and fed the patients who couldn't feed themselves. We scrubbed and sterilised bedpans, packed the sterilisers, made dressings, cottonwool swabs and sanitary napkins, cleaned the ward, changed dressings, mopped up vomit, urine and faeces, gave enemas, washed and bathed patients and delivered and dispensed the medications. One trainee was always a runner between the wards to cover the breaks. On each ward a nurse and a trainee would have to report to Sister on the names and status of up to thirty-five patients.

'There was very little bombing in our area but when the sirens went we had to fill all the baths and basins with water and prepare to evacuate. It was the hardest work you can imagine. And you were expected to go to lectures in your free time, irrespective of whether you were on day or night shifts. We had to put up the blackout and take it down again. We were maids as well as nurses, scattering dried tea-leaves on the ward floors every day to lay the dust before we swept the floors. Often your days off were cancelled if things got very busy. So it's not surprising that when the war was declared a lot of the girls left and went to work in the munitions factories, which was pretty hard work too but shorter hours and better paid.'

Moira stayed on and qualified as a State Registered Nurse because she wanted a career, and by the time war ended she was ready to find an area of specialisation. 'I wanted to travel the world and see places. I didn't like theatre work, and I didn't like dealing with babies so maternity wasn't for me. I wanted to be able to look after long-term patients, people I could get to know,' she explains. 'I don't remember how I first heard about East Grinstead, I think someone just told me that Archibald McIndoe was looking for nurses that wanted to specialise in plastic surgery. I thought that would be wonderful because plastic surgery was fairly new and everyone thought there was a great future in it, so I applied to Mr McIndoe's maxillo-facial unit.'

Moira moved to East Grinstead in 1945, full of hope and enthusiasm, but was initially shocked by coming face to face with the chronic injuries and horrifying facial disfigurement of the Guinea Pigs. 'It wasn't easy at first but Mr McIndoe was adamant that you had to appear as though everything was normal and not ever look as though you minded. I remember him saying, "If those boys see you look at them as though they're repugnant, you're finished here because you'll set my work back months, maybe forever." But you learn to see beyond the disfigurement, and it happens quite quickly so that I soon found I was seeing the person rather than just the terrible damage.'

To Moira, working on Ward III was 'heaven' after the torturous years in Harrogate. 'Everyone was very friendly, even Matron and the doctors, everyone was on Christian name terms. A lot of the sisters where I trained were really horrible, quite sadistic, they seemed to delight in withholding praise or even approval and you'd be punished for the smallest thing. So East Grinstead was marvellous. You had the feeling that everyone was working together, although we were all very clear that Mr McIndoe was in charge and he was a hard taskmaster. He was never rude or condescending though—I never called him Archie but a lot of people did, and Archie was God.'

By 1946 Moira was working mainly on nights. I ask her about the bad language, the slack behaviour and practical jokes that had so offended some members of the hospital board. She smiles and changes the conversation to something else, but later we return to it. 'Wasn't this hard for the nurses?' I ask.

She hesitates. 'These men were heroes,' she says, 'at heart they were lovely, and they were our boys, and so brave. But they got away with quite a lot.'

I repeat the question and Moira puts down her cup and looks away. 'They were high-spirited, they had wonderful spirits really when you think of what happened to them. They helped each other, and they helped us too, folding linen, helping in the sluice, feeding each other. We were all part of a team. It wasn't always easy, especially if I thought back to all I'd been taught in training about keeping your distance, and discipline and so on. If they went out at night and came home a bit the worse for wear, I'd sit them down in the kitchen, make them coffee and maybe some toast and a poached egg, and calm them down. You have to remember that by the time I went there the war was almost over. That had an effect on them; from what I heard things were more ... let's say ... boisterous during the war.'

This makes sense to me: although the injuries remained, the tension of the war was alleviated, the British were still riding a wave of relief , and the postwar slump of spirits in the later 40s had not yet set in.

'And was that a general feeling among the nurses?' I ask. 'Were they largely okay with the way the men behaved?'

There's a longish silence and then Moira shrugs. 'Some of the young and experienced ones didn't cope so well. It was one of the best experiences of my life. My time at East Grinstead was a wonderfully unique experience. Sir Archibald and his boys were remarkable people.'

A few years later Moira left Ward III to work in a plastic surgery ward in Stockholm. It was the first stage of her plan to travel the world, but she hadn't got very far when in 1952 she met Sir Frank Nelson, a former Conservative Member of Parliament who had been appointed by the War Cabinet as chief of the Special Operations Executive (SOE) on its creation in July 1940. Nelson, at that time, was energetic and physically strong and he threw himself wholeheartedly into the job of establishing the new and secret department, with a charter of almost limitless scope. This brief in itself aroused hostility throughout Whitehall and he daily battled both veiled and overt animosity. Two years later he had, through force of character, managed to get his organisation accepted and recognised as an essential development in modern warfare, and he had also established a reputation for honesty and complete unselfishness. But by then the SOE and his earlier total commitment to his work in Parliament and diplomatic service overseas had ruined his health. He retired in 1942 at the age of fifty-nine and was rewarded with a knighthood soon after. Some years later his first wife, Jean, with whom he had a son, died, and in 1952 he met and married Moira Carling. He was sixty-nine and she was very much younger. 'We were very happy,' Moira says, 'he was a wonderful man, but he was always unrealistic about money, which is why I'm living on just my pension. He never had to pay contributions, never made any provision for the future. He just never thought about those sorts of things.' She nursed him with great devotion until he died in 1966. 'I'm a long-time widow,' she says. 'Forty-one years and counting.'

*

I drive out of Oxford early that evening with the sense that I have missed an opportunity. This might have been the breakthrough I needed but I have failed to probe potentially difficult issues, and may have missed a vital chance to learn more about Moira's time at East Grinstead and what was happening among the other nurses. It's not simply that I liked and admired Moira Nelson, but her manner—her way of being—catapulted me back to childhood, to my parents and grandparents, the nuns at the convent where I went to school, to the England of the 50s, right into the heart of that idea which I have been chasing, of a very different time and place. I've felt this too with the Guinea Pigs; I am reluctant to ask the questions that might rock their boat and intrude on sensitive issues. So I have held back because here, in this country with these people, genuine curiosity and enquiry feel like an intrusion. I know I inherited my parents' respect for authority, a respect that sometimes seemed to verge on fear. And for me authority almost always appeared in the form of an older man. At home it was my father and his friends. At school it was the nuns of course, but the final authority who reduced those strong, intelligent women to submissive ciphers was Father Parfitt, the elderly priest who appeared each week and had them scuttling into corners, or walking behind him at a respectful distance.

There have been times in my life when I have been very good at asking difficult questions, particularly at needling politicians and bureaucrats, face to face, as a broadcaster and in writing, but not in this situation and not in this country. It starts to rain again and I head gloomily towards Woodstock where I have booked an overnight stay in a pub.

Later, I lie on the bed under a sloping roof looking out over the sodden landscape trying to work out why, in pursuing a project on which I've long dreamed of embarking, I'm proving so ineffective, and feeling so pathetic. After the first few days of enthusiasm and energy I have been trapped by this sense of inadequacy, enchanted by the idea of the past but paralysed by it. In the last four or five years the idea of England as home has been uncomfortably strong, tugging at my emotions, causing me to weep copiously at depictions of village life, in re-runs of *All Creatures Great and Small* or *Midsomer Murders*. I am still reaching out for that, and when I glimpse aspects of it, as I did with Moira this afternoon, I feel disabled by it. I become a child again, trying to conform to all those confusing, unspoken rules and expectations, silenced by the power of the past, by all that I know about being a nice, middle-class convent girl, in the conservative Home Counties in 50s England: compliant, respectful, accepting, and knowing exactly when the moment comes to stop asking difficult questions.

My parents came from traditionally working-class families in the East End of London, and were quite typical of many who had struggled up into the middle-class and aimed higher, not because they desired flashy demonstrations of wealth, but to acquire, in my father's case in particular, I believe, a sense of authority. As they struggled on up they constantly looked back down in fear of losing their footing. They were people who knew they would never wield power but understood that it was the recognition and performance of authority that mattered. That distinction seems peculiarly English. It was not taken for granted that possessing power necessarily entitled a person to use it. Authority, on the other hand, allowed one to question the exercise of power. Privacy mattered, as did the right to own your space, and the right to close your door and do as you wished behind it because that was nobody else's business. It was unseemly to talk about what you owned or earned. It was even more unseemly to talk about one's feelings, and worse still to ask intrusive questions.

Now the British spill their emotional guts on television every day. Reality TV spies on the most extreme, the extraordinary, the most embarrassing and intimate, and the most banal examples of human behaviour. Chat-show hosts probe every facet of what used to be private life. In cafés and restaurants, on trains and buses, people talk loudly to each other or into their phones about their relationships, their partners, parents, children, their bosses and colleagues, their financial affairs and their sex lives. The characteristic English reserve has, for generations younger than my own, dissolved, to be replaced by a desire to make every thing public. Of course much of this is also true of Australia, but here in England it seems like an offence to everything I am trying to recover from the past.

One thing that's clear to me is that older people have changed very little. Indeed for many I suspect their reserve has strengthened with the desire to protect their physical and emotional space against the threat of the invasion of privacy. My dilemma is that I admire that reserve and want to respect it, but at the same time not only do I want the Guinea Pigs to reveal much more, I also want to uncover stories of the nurses.

11. CONNECTIONS

The following morning I wake hung-over by my own failure. Alone in the small dining room of the pub I order wholemeal toast, Marmite and English Breakfast tea and am waiting for it to arrive, staring out of the window and wondering whether it will rain again, when a devastatingly handsome young man in chef's whites appears at my table.

'You 'ave ordered toast, Madame, but I am come to tell you that I 'ave just baked the fresh croissants and perhaps you prefer to 'ave ...'

'Definitely,' I say. 'I would love fresh croissants and change the tea to coffee please.' He gives me a beautiful smile, disappears into the kitchen returning seconds later with three enormous, piping hot croissants in a basket. Thank heavens for the EU and what it has done for British catering. It's remarkable what a freshly baked croissant or three can do for one's mood.

Back in my room I decide to follow up the contacts Moira has given me for some former nurses. It's a long time since she was in touch with them, she'd said, but they may still be on these numbers. I dial the first number and a woman answers—her mother, she tells me, died a few months ago and she is clearing out her house. 'Can I help with anything?'

I explain why I'm calling and ask whether her mother ever talked about her time as a nurse at East Grinstead, or perhaps kept any journals. 'Mum never talked about it much,' she says. 'Really only ever mentioned how wonderful Mr McIndoe was, and how brave the pilots were. I often tried to get her to talk more about the war but she always said she preferred to let things lie. She lost two brothers and her fiancé so the war was a very sad time for her.'

I thank her, cross her mother's name off the list and dial the next number, which proves to be no longer in service. On to the third, and it rings for a while before a woman answers rather fiercely. 'Yes, that's me,' she says when I confirm her name. 'What do you want?'

I explain what I'm doing and that I'd like to talk to her about her time at East Grinstead. 'I'm sick of all that,' she says, or rather shouts. 'I don't want to go back over it. It's all in the past. Don't call again.' And she slams down the phone.

I am left now with just one lead on a nurse, a contact emailed to me by a friend just before I left the studio. But for now I have to get back on the road. I begin stuffing my things into my bag. Today I'm heading to Witney to meet another Guinea Pig, Dennis Neale. I'm making my way out of my room when my mobile rings and I dump my things on the bed while I answer it.

'It's Angela,' a voice says. 'From Victoria Station, we talked about the Guinea Pigs. Do you remember?'

I had completely forgotten this encounter that took place when I had just missed a train back to East Grinstead after one of my early visits to the Imperial War Museum. With more than half an hour to wait I went to one of the cafés for a coffee. The tables were all taken so I picked a small one where a woman about my own age was sitting reading. I asked if she minded if I took the other chair and she gestured to me to sit down, and I did so, putting my coffee and my own book on the table. It was a second-hand copy of Leonard Mosley's *Faces From the Fire*, the biography of Archibald McIndoe, with a large black and white photo of the surgeon on its now rather tattered dustcover.

The woman leaned forward and tapped the cover with her finger. 'The Guinea Pig man,' she said. 'My uncle was a Guinea Pig.'

I was taken aback. When I tell people I'm doing research for a book on the Guinea Pig Club they usually assume it's group of cavy enthusiasts and give me a funny look. Her name, she said, was Angela, and McIndoe treated her uncle in 1943. When I asked her if she thought I might be able to interview him she grimaced. 'I doubt it, he's a sort of dissenter, so he generally doesn't say much.'

'A dissenter?'

'Mmm. He gave up on it all a long time ago, the fifties I think.'

A Guinea Pig who gave up on the club sounded fascinating, but she seemed to know very little about it. 'I'd love to talk to a dissenter,' I said, and explained I was also trying to find nurses.

'Can't help you there,' she said, and we talked more about the war and then about England and Australia, both of us watching the indicator so we'd know which platform to head for. Her train was due ahead of mine and eventually she gathered her things together and said how nice it had been to talk.

'Do you think your uncle might be willing to talk to me?' I asked again. 'It can be off the record and I wouldn't have to use his name.'

Angela hesitated. 'I don't know,' she'd said, as I'd scrawled my number on a card and handed it to her. 'I'll ask him if you like, but he doesn't talk about it much, so I wouldn't hold your breath.'

For the next few days I jumped every time the phone rang, hoping for the mysterious dissenting uncle, but he never called.

'I talked to my uncle,' Angela says now. 'He lives near Brighton. He said he'd like to meet you but he'd like me to be there.'

I suggest a day the following week and ask for the address.

'He wants to meet you at the hospital,' Angela says. 'He'd like to have a look around. It's years since he was there. So if it's all right with you I'll drive us up and we'll meet you there. There must be a café where we could meet and talk.'

I explain that Ward III, where her uncle would have been treated, is now the café, and she might want to check whether he's okay with going there. We make a date and she says she call back if he'd prefer to meet elsewhere. I thank her profusely and she laughs. 'I'm amazed,' she says. 'He said no at first, and then changed his mind. But he may not be able to tell you anything you don't already know, we might just be wasting your time.'

'I'll take my chance,' I say and we hang up.

A meeting with a dissenting Guinea Pig, whatever dissenting means, is intriguing, and revives my spirits enormously. I pay my bill at the pub and am putting my bag into the boot of the car when the gorgeous chef comes out into the car park waving to me. 'There is no person to eat the croissants,' he says. 'But I see you like them ...' and he presses a brown paper bag into my hand and disappears back inside. The bag contains three still-warm croissants, a plastic knife, several individual portions of butter and jam and some paper napkins. It's good to know that I am shallow enough to have my self-esteem restored by fresh croissants and the prospect of a little intrigue. It's about to rain again but I am feeling quite sunny as I head off on the road to Witney to meet Guinea Pig Dennis Neale and his wife Eunice.

*

I had allowed half an hour to drive to Witney and then added another half hour for traffic but today it's not the traffic but the rain that slows me down. It seems to fall in buckets, hitting the ground with such force that the water rebounds in a blinding mist. Several times the visibility is so poor that I have to stop and wait for it to ease before going on. Eventually I make it to Witney and try to follow Dennis's instructions to get to his home. There I lose myself several times, unable to read the street signs. Finally I pull into the narrow parking space in front of a row of shops and call Dennis. I'm very close he tells me, he'll come and get me, and before I can stop him he has hung up. A few minutes later a car draws alongside mine and I let down my window. Dennis is immediately recognisable—even among the Guinea Pigs, eyes located at very different levels on the face are uncommon, but in that first glance I also have a strong and uncanny feeling that we have met before. Is this the man from the staircase? But no, this is something else.

'Follow me, it's not far,' Dennis calls from his open window as we set off at a crawl, and a few minutes later we are shaking the rain off us and removing our shoes in the hallway of the Neale's home, while Eunice puts the kettle on.

'Now you can see why the boys call me Dennis "Eyes Higher" Neale,' he says, hanging up his raincoat. 'One eye's very much higher than the other.'

It is indeed—about an inch higher—and yet he has a handsome face, less surprising than many others. He is a tall, very upright man with a strong presence and a gentle manner. Before meeting any of the Guinea Pigs I've studied photographs of them taken before, during and after their reconstruction at East Grinstead, and many of them photographed again recently, but this instant sense of recognition is something I haven't felt before.

We make ourselves comfortable in the lounge and Eunice comes in to tell us the tea is on its way.

'Forgive me if I've forgotten this,' Dennis says, 'but I feel as though we've met before.'

'I have that feeling too,' I say. But we quickly establish that we have never met.

He smiles. 'Odd, isn't it. I want to say perhaps it was in another life, but that sort of thing makes some people uneasy.'

'Sounds right to me,' I say as Eunice appears from the kitchen with a tray of tea.

Dennis was just fifteen when he joined the RAF in 1935, and when the war began he was assigned to Bomber Command as a wireless operator. In January 1943, as part of a secret squadron on a night mission patrolling the English Channel near the north coast of France, he was in the turret of the first of three Defiance aircraft flying with reduced lighting. The pilot had virtually no vision, and was relying on Dennis to direct him from the turret. They landed safely, the second aircraft followed, but the third missed the spot and landed on top of Dennis's.

'So I'm a total Guinea Pig,' he says, 'because I was mashed, boiled *and* fried. And the metal propeller cut off parts of my face. Apparently I was very belligerent. I tried to punch the man who rescued me, and I had to have military police on either side of me when I was on the stretcher. Our mission had been secret and they were afraid I'd start talking–rambling.'

Dennis was taken to Chichester where Archibald McIndoe, on his round of RAF hospitals, saw him a couple of days later and had him transferred immediately to East Grinstead. Dennis remembers none of this except a moment in the ambulance when he heard a woman say she was hungry and ask the driver to stop at a cake shop. There was a conversation about how many currant buns were wanted. Someone prodded Dennis and then called out, 'Don't worry about him, he won't last the journey.' The next thing he knew was when he regained consciousness just before arriving at East Grinstead.

'I asked the lovely nurse from the ambulance, who'd been with me all the time, if she'd enjoyed the currant buns, and she was horrified that I'd overheard.'

Dennis's catalogue of injuries was daunting: his olfactory bone was broken off, his top jaw was in two pieces, bottom jaw in three, his nasal bone had penetrated the roof of his mouth and his right eye was hanging on his cheek. His mother was told that his chance of survival was fifty-fifty. McIndoe performed numerous operations including rebuilding the roof of Dennis's mouth, and he took lumps of bone from his right hip to replace the nose bone. 'I still have one hip more prominent than the other and my belt keeps slipping down,' he says with a smile. By the end of the war McIndoe was still working on Dennis's face, which was bandaged for many months with just slits left for his eyes, and a wire holding his jaw in place.

He recalls that while his face and eyes were completely bandaged his bed was whizzed across the ward towed by someone on a bike, and he talks about the exceptional camaraderie, and the unusual freedom at East Grinstead. 'You didn't talk about what you'd been through, unless it was to joke about it,' he says. 'There was always someone worse off than you, but we were all in it together, and knowing that, and having Archie there kept us going. In a way the ward was a bit like a private club—most things were allowed as long as you didn't upset the nurses or the medical people. The nurses were wonderful, but if one shuddered at the sight of us she was shown the door pretty quickly. We got away with a lot because Archie thought we had suffered more than anyone should have to. And you know, despite all that, we were all waiting to get back to flying.'

I ask him if being with others who had similarly horrific experiences made it unnecessary to actually talk about how it felt. 'Yes, well I think so, as I said, we'd refer to it—to things that happened in a jokey way, I suppose you'd call it fatalistic and self-deprecating.'

'And what about the nurses? Do you think that they might've had a hard time of it with all the teasing and the practical jokes.'

'Well I didn't think so then,' Dennis says, 'but you probably wouldn't get away with that these days. For us it was fun and it helped us to feel like men again. But some time ago, at one of the reunions, I was talking to a nurse and she told me she was very unhappy there because she felt bullied, and nurses couldn't complain because Archie was so much for his boys. So she probably wasn't the only one who felt that way.'

Eunice has left the room to answer the door so I take a deep breath and pluck up my courage. 'So do you think there could have been some sexual coercion?'

Dennis looks straight at me. 'Not on my part,' he says, 'although I won't say it wasn't tempting. As for the others I can't say, but boys will be boys.'

This is the first time I've heard this sort of acknowledgement and then there's another first. Dennis starts to talk unprompted, about facial disfigurement, in other than humorous or superficial terms.

'Archie taught us a lot. "No matter how you look," he used to say, "don't ever stop recognising who you are." He taught us to accept ourselves as complete human beings, it took some time for that to sink in because even when you know there are no more operations and you look in the mirror, you're still not seeing the man you were. There's someone different there, and he's nothing like as good looking as you. I kept wanting to get myself back, and hoping to see what I remembered instead of what was really in front of me.'

Dennis pauses and looks away, his cup and saucer rattle in his shaking hand, and he clears his throat. Eunice, who has just rejoined us, nods reassuringly which I assume means I should wait and not try to fill the silence, which is now uncomfortably long. And he finally takes a deep breath, turns back to us and puts his cup down on the table.

'It's very hard to go out in the world with a Guinea Pig face,' he says, 'it's not only how you feel about yourself, but it affects other people, it makes them uneasy. And there's how they behave to you. They attach ideas about your personality to your face and it's often completely wrong. Some people think that having a damaged face means you're wrong in the head. People were really ignorant then and we copped that ignorance. They'd stare at us and nudge each other and whisper, as though we couldn't see or understand what they were doing. It's terrible to see that people are frightened of you, especially when it's children and they hide their faces or start crying. I don't think people knew what an effect that can have, when you feel them looking at you. It's worse than all the pain and the operations because you know you have to live the rest of your life with this face, no escape from that. You get used to it or you don't and I know some of the fellows didn't.

'Archie warned us about it and tried to prepare us for it, although nothing prepares you really. We were lucky in East Grinstead because he made the people accept us. It was safe for us to go out, people didn't stare or laugh or whisper, they'd smile as though they knew us. We were sort of merged into the town. Archie did that. But everywhere else it was totally different and that went on for a long time, long after the war.

'Archie taught us to have confidence in spite of everything. And he said that embarrassment started with us ourselves. "So if someone is looking at you and seems embarrassed it's because they are picking up that embarrassment from you. Don't let that happen, act as though nothing's wrong. There is nothing wrong with being a war hero," he said.'

I ask him how he feels about his face now and whether he is angry about what happened to him.

He shrugs. 'I've got used to it. And people are better these days, it's not like it was then. Sometimes when I'm shaving I still stop and look at myself in the mirror and ask—why me? But I'm not angry, no point; who could I be angry with? I was lucky to be at East Grinstead and to have the Guinea Pig Club. I wouldn't change it. Not any of it.'

After the war Dennis returned to the RAF as a Warrant Officer at a base in Germany although he was unable to fly. He dreamed of running a pub and some years later that dream came true when he and his first wife took over The Red Lion in Cassington. Eventually he moved to Witney to work for blanket makers, Charles Early, where he met Eunice. 'She was full of fun and very down to earth,' Dennis says, 'and she had a heart full of empathy, and that's what I needed. Empathy not sympathy.'

'I used to get very angry when people looked at Dennis in a funny way,' Eunice says. 'I wanted to tell them off, because he is such a wonderful person, I wanted to make them understand. But he never gets angry, he just takes everything in his stride.'

Dennis nods. 'The outcome of it all is that I'm a fatalist. I have no fear of death at all. It goes back to knowing that I was fifty-fifty, that I could fall either side of the line. I'm eighty-seven and I appreciate life, I don't think about age. I live each day for itself.'

By the time I leave the Neales' home that afternoon the rain has stopped and the sun is making an effort. Dennis's story is probably no worse and no better than that of many of the other men I've met but that sense of connection has intensified my response to it. We had parted speaking of meeting again when they come to East Grinstead for the Guinea Pig reunion dinner. When we do meet, in that room full of people clinking glasses, laughing and talking, Eunice tells me that Dennis has just been diagnosed with leukaemia. When it's time to leave Dennis hugs me.

'I hope I'll see you again,' he says, 'but I don't think I'll be here much longer, so maybe in yet another life.' Just six weeks later I hear that he is gone. I only met Dennis twice, once at his home in Witney in July, and then briefly at the reunion dinner in October. I spent only a few hours with him, but the loss seems as great as if I'd known him for much longer.

12. DOING YOUR BIT FOR THE WAR

The day after I get back to Hartfield from Oxfordshire I decide to follow up on the contact my oldest friend Evelyn had given me just before I left. Evelyn and I have known each other for more than fifty years, but most of that time only at a distance. We were firm friends as children and teenagers, living opposite each other on the outskirts of a village, far away from other friends. But we drifted apart in our early twenties: different interests, different jobs, then marriage and children, and for me, eventually, another country. But a few years ago I managed to find her through the website Friends Reunited. Fortuitously, it was at a time when she was planning a holiday in Australia. And so we had met, a few months later, in Perth, and the years disappeared. Evelyn was just as I knew her as a young woman – only older, wiser, and even more independent and strong minded.

'I'm not sure you should be doing this Guinea Pig thing,' she had said when I first arrived in England. 'I mean it's almost sacred territory isn't it. And you're just an outsider. You weren't born 'til forty-four, I don't understand why you want to do it.'

While we share a childhood, our backgrounds and our interests are totally different. Evelyn grew up in harsh conditions: a run-down cottage on a few acres of land with some chickens, ducks and geese, some pigs and one cow, barely subsistence for a couple with two daughters. Her father had some casual work trimming hedges, digging ditches; her mother cleaned houses. Evelyn left school at sixteen and went to work for the Inland Revenue, then married and started her own very successful retail business, which she later developed into a small chain of outlets and finally sold only a few years ago. My parents were reasonably well off and I also left school at sixteen, started life as a secretary, then drifted into journalism, writing, and later academia. So we come to this subject from different perspectives and very different political positions. We clash on many things but always manage to rise above the difference.

Explaining my motivation has been difficult, largely because Evelyn doesn't understand why I need to unpack the men's stories, and even less why I want to find the nurses. And she is not trapped by how things used to be because she has lived with the changing culture of this country as it happened. She can do nostalgia, but she knows that's all it is. She also remembers the Guinea Pigs, in some cases better than I do, as she is two years older and, unlike me, had no fear of them. She thinks I am on a fool's errand. Her down-to-earth approach has been helpful as it makes me try to articulate my motivation. And her scepticism has actually made me more determined to keep going. So I was surprised when she had called to tell me that at a reunion dinner for local business owners she had been talking about my project to a man who had then told her that his aunt had nursed the Guinea Pigs.

'So he gave me her number,' Evelyn had said. 'Don't know if it's any use. Her name is Joyce*.'

'Yes, my brother told me you might call,' Joyce says on the phone. 'I can tell you a bit about working at the hospital but it's a long way for you to come. I might not be able to tell you anything you don't already know.'

In fact it's about seventy kilometres from Hartfield to Canterbury and the next day I set out in glorious sunshine through the Kent and Sussex countryside, hoping again that this is a breakthrough and that I won't lose my nerve.

Much has been written about the liberating effect of the war for women: the increased sexual freedom, and the opening up of opportunities for work and training in areas which, before the war, were exclusively male. But more recent oral histories of women's wartime lives have led some researchers to question the official and popular construction of the Second World War as a period of heightened sexual opportunity and activity. Rather than seeing this as a time of liberation when sexual inhibitions were abandoned, a growing number of historians now interpret the war as a period in which conformity to traditional constructions of femininity and female sexual behaviour remained comparatively unchanged.[42] Also questioned is the image of the Second World War as a time in which 'altruism, character and service' created a society united 'by a coherent sense of purpose', as suggested in a social history of the war published in 1958.[43] More recent research indicates that 'the effect of wartime mobilization may have been to provoke a retreat into the private sphere' and that 'people did what they could to preserve the integrity of their private lives against the relentless disruptions of war—evacuation, military and industrial conscription'.[44]

Penny Summerfield and Nicole Crocket write of the 'evidence of men's coercive sexual behaviour' during the war, including for example 'seducing young women on the grounds that a soldier might die tomorrow'. They point to feminist readings of the wartime destabilisation of sexual relations that suggest that 'the disruption of war could be seen as stimulating men to assert their sexual authority'.[45] This seems significant in relation to the experience of nurses at East Grinstead, who were working in a traditionally female occupation, in male-occupied territory, and under the authority of a male surgeon who wanted the best for his patients, whatever the cost. In this case, part of what McIndoe believed to be the best thing for his men was the close proximity of attractive, compliant women. While the men laugh off their individual and collective behaviour as fun and games, or harmless teasing and pranks, I find it hard to believe that this describes the experience of all the nurses.

Women were subjected to a plethora of confusing messages both about their sexuality and their role in the war. Wartime propaganda frequently circulated verbal and visual messages that implied that fascism was a direct threat to women. They were widely depicted as the casualties of potential bombings, or as victims of the evil Hun or the murdering Japanese who would capture, rape and kill them. Images of women in this propaganda were often highly eroticised. Indeed, the advent of war seems to have sparked a general increase in the eroticising of women, not just as victims but also as a source of danger to the fighting man and to national security. War itself was frequently depicted as a disease-ridden whore luring young men to their death in the footsteps of their fathers. Women were also implicated as potentially dangerous in other ways. A poster in the collection at the Imperial War Museum shows a glamorous blonde in evening dress, surrounded by admiring servicemen, with the message *Keep mum—she's not so dumb! Careless talk costs lives,* positioning the woman as at least a risk and at worst a spy. So too does another in the 'careless talk costs lives' series, in which a cartoon of two women talking over tea and cakes is accompanied by the message *Don't forget walls have ears.* The wallpaper in the background is made up of multiple line drawings of Hitler's face.

Posters designed to recruit women into the armed services or to work in the factories were framed in terms of service to the war effort and particularly in support of fighting men. In an RAF recruiting poster, a woman in uniform looks upward into the middle distance, behind her is a pilot wearing a flying helmet and goggles, and behind them is the flag of the RAF. *Serve in the WAAF with the Men who Fly* is the recruiting message. Similarly, a navy recruitment poster shows a woman in uniform, looking out to sea, with the message *Join The Wrens and Free a Man for the Fleet.* And *Women of Britain Come into the Factories* is the call on another, with an illustration of a smiling woman in overalls looking upwards, arms outstretched against the silhouette of factory chimneys, a fleet of aircraft climbing into the skies above her. Almost without exception, recruiting posters for the services used photographs or drawings of beautiful women smiling into the middle distance rather than looking into the camera. Most nursing recruitment posters also show glamourised images of young women in crisp uniforms, once again smiling nobly into the distance. One interesting exception uses a photograph of a pleasant-looking, but certainly not glamorous, nurse in uniform superimposed on an equally unglamorous row of hospital beds and patients: *Make Nursing Your War Job—it's War Work with a Future.*

Meanwhile, these idealised images of women's war work contrasted with the eroticised images of women in partial service uniforms or overalls but with buttons undone to partially reveal breasts, or simply without the skirt or trousers to display many fine pairs of legs. These images on calendars and posters were displayed in the service canteens, industrial workshops, where women were now part of the workforce. And in support of the domestic situation, women at home with young children were pictured as youthful, angelic and vulnerable, alongside messages that defined their protection as what the war was being fought for. Beauty was central to the image of women; in fact the writer and BBC broadcaster J. B. Priestley coined the phrase 'beauty is duty' for women in wartime: angelic, disciplined idealistic beauty at work; beauty and purity in homemaking and motherhood; and beauty plus sexiness everywhere else.

While young women without children were subject to call up, and recruiting posters depicted heroic occupations, many found that they were constantly directed to positions in which their role was simply to serve and support the men in the armed services and in reserved occupations. Once in those jobs, women were often met with mistrust and hostility from men who saw their presence and their competence as a threat to gender stability. In some cases this even resulted in the sabotage of women's work, with reports of male workers adding sugar to the petrol in engines, or loosening screws in vehicle or aircraft factories after the woman had signed off her part of the job.

James Hinton, searching for sources of active citizenship in the wartime diaries kept as part of the Mass Observation project, comments that 'wider themes emerged' in these records. In women's diaries in particular he found he was reading about 'individual struggles for personal autonomy'.[46]

Many women were drawn to work that was entirely different from what they had ever thought possible. They relished the challenge, the danger, the hard slog of meaningful work and the chance to work alongside male peers, although many were disappointed that their role was always to support the men who had the more challenging and exciting jobs. But others preferred to stay in or join up for traditionally female occupations and many nurses fell into this category. Some trained nurses signed up for the forces, while others opted to nurse on the home front. For these and other women who served in various capacities in nursing, the services and the factories on the home front, danger was always present. Unlike the previous war, the home front in this one was a very dangerous place to be.

Wherever it was done, nursing was exhausting, back-breaking work with long hours and high levels of professional and emotional stress. But for many women it was their chosen way of doing their bit for the war. It was also a way in which enthusiastic young women managed to escape the restrictions of anxious or controlling parents. The traditionally 'feminine' nature of nursing fitted with the image of women as carers, as givers and supporters of life, as nurturers and comforters. This satisfied many an anxious father who would have laid down the law about a daughter in battledress servicing aircraft engines. While a few certainly reacted to the prospect of a daughter having intimate access to male bodies, most parents seem to have viewed nursing as a respectable, even ladylike, occupation. Reality was, of course, somewhat different; much nursing work was hard domestic slog in very poor conditions. While images of beautiful women in crisp uniforms wiping the brows of handsome wounded heroes were attractive to parents and their daughters alike, it was a far cry from the constant emptying of bedpans, clearing up vomit, cleaning and dressing suppurating wounds, administering enemas, washing and dressing dead bodies, and facing horrific injuries.

*

Joyce lives in a chocolate-box cottage on the outskirts of Canterbury. It has white lathe and plaster walls, a deep thatched roof, and diamond-paned leadlight windows. The garden is a riot of colour: hollyhocks, foxgloves, sweet williams, roses and lavender.

'It's a very sheltered spot,' Joyce says when I comment on how well the plants have survived the last few weeks of appalling weather. 'We've been lucky. My mother would have been in heaven here. She had a biscuit tin with a picture of a thatched cottage on the lid, and she dreamed of living somewhere like this.'

Joyce was sixteen and living with her mother and five younger siblings in the East End of London when war was declared. She had left school at fourteen and worked in a small draper's shop. In 1940, following her seventeenth birthday, she volunteered for nursing, did the basic Red Cross VAD training and was sent to East Grinstead.

'I had to leave Mum alone with the others. I was five years older than my next brother, and my youngest sister was only six and was consumptive. It was a lot of work for Mum. My dad died in a fire at the factory where he worked, early in nineteen thirty-nine. So I felt very bad about leaving Mum, but I was secretly excited. Ever since I was a little girl I wanted to be a nurse.'

We talk more generally about the war, the recruitment of women and Joyce's own optimism about nursing. 'I was very naïve,' she tells me. 'Never had a boyfriend. Mum and Dad were quite religious, we all went to chapel on Sundays. Mum was very worried about me getting into some kind of trouble so even at sixteen she was very strict about what I could do and where I could go. So that was the other thing, volunteering felt very grown up. I was excited about it.'

Joyce goes on to talk about arriving at East Grinstead and the shock of her first encounters with the patients on Ward III. 'I could barely believe it—men with no noses or chins, the first man I saw had one good eye and a hole where the other one used to be. The hands were awful—just stumps and lumps. And those pedicles, they frightened the life out of me.'

But she was surprised at how quickly she became immune to appearances and was able to relate to the men themselves rather than to how they looked. 'They were very brave, you couldn't help but admire them.'

'So you got on all right with the patients?' I ask and I tell her that from what I read and heard from Guinea Pigs themselves I imagine it could have been a pretty difficult environment to work in. 'The whole atmosphere, not just the nursing itself, seems to have made a lot of extra demands on the nurses,' I venture.

Joyce shrugs, and looks away. 'It certainly did,' she says, getting up and saying, decisively, that it's time for a cup of tea. My heart sinks; once again I've hit a wall. But this time I am not going to give up. Joyce returns with the tea and I manage to steer the conversation back to the Ward and McIndoe's approach to treatment, the outings and social events he organised for patients.

'Did you get involved in those?' I ask.

Joyce leans forward, lowering her voice although she's already told me that we are alone in the house. 'I don't know how much you know about this,' she says, 'but it was ... well an unusual situation.'

I tell her about the conversation at The Hedgehog, and what I've read about Ward III. She relaxes, sits back and gives me a long, searching look.

'I've never talked about it,' she says, 'it seems disloyal to the men. A lot of them were lovely, I don't want to say anything that ... that makes them sound bad.'

I wait in silence and then she straightens up in her chair.

'I don't have happy memories of East Grinstead,' she says, 'I was so ignorant that it scared me. I couldn't stop thinking what my mother would say. She'd have been horrified and I knew I'd never be able to tell her about it. I'd left her alone to do my bit for the war, and neither of us had any idea ... well, I was only seventeen. I knew it would be hard work, and the patients would have nasty injuries, but I didn't expect ... it was naïve, I can see that now but I didn't think about having to deal with men's private parts. Imagine the shock, I'd never seen a penis and in my first week I had to change a dressing on one. So I didn't only see my first penis but by the time I'd finished with it I'd seen the first erect one! I can laugh about it now and all nurses have to get used to that sort of thing. But I didn't know *anything* about sex. I didn't know how you ... well how people did it. I did ask Mum once how you got pregnant and she went bright red and said, "You'll find out soon enough." 'Til I got to East Grinstead I honestly thought you could only get pregnant if you were married. I know it's hard to believe but there were a lot of girls like me then. No one told us anything.

'And then when I got there ... well ... the war was the excuse and explanation for everything. You did what you could for the war effort. I was green as anything. Oh you've no idea. Well I learnt more in my first month there than I'd learned in the whole of the rest of my life, and it wasn't all about nursing. I was really shaken when I saw it, all the flirting, you know, and the teasing. I wasn't the sort of girl who was used to that. I didn't know how to stand up for myself, and the men, they'd be acting familiar, like you were their girlfriend. I'd not had any experience with men. It was very hard on us. You were being pushed into putting up with things you wouldn't put up with from anyone else, and that were really embarrassing, and ... well ... not nice. The language and the jokes, the way they talked to you. Sometimes they'd try and kiss you or put their arms round you, maybe sneak up behind you and whirl you round.

'I didn't know how to behave. Some of the girls ... there was quite a lot of sex went on—and it was always in the air, if you know what I mean. So every day, going to work, you knew you'd not only have to do your job, but you'd have to cope with that. There was always someone trying to coax you into getting friendly or more than that ... and some of them ... they'd laugh at you and call you snooty or other things. I was ashamed of being so ignorant, and ashamed as though it was my fault. I didn't know what to do. And you couldn't complain because Mr McIndoe, he ... well ... he thought it was good for them.

'I don't think he understood how it was for some of us

girls. There were others like me, but knowing that didn't help much because all of what was happening was quite divisive. I know some didn't mind, they'd go into the operating theatre at night with a man and ... Well anyway I know of one, she was a VAD like me, she went home for a couple of days off and never came back, someone said she was pregnant and was frightened about what her parents would say. I never heard what happened to her. And one nurse had a breakdown and left, but she came back and had another breakdown and went home and didn't come back that time. And I remember one of the older nurses being very upset because she was married and her husband was away in the army, and she kept saying, "What would Eddie say if he knew?" because she was worried he'd think she'd been leading them on. Now that I'm older and understand it better and I can see that it would've helped for them to think that women wanted to be with them in that way. But I couldn't make sense of anything back then. It was just, head down, grit my teeth and hope I could get through the day.'

I ask Joyce why she didn't leave, or ask to be transferred elsewhere.

'I wanted to but I didn't know how. It's hard to complain about things that other people seem to think is okay, and Mr McIndoe was ... rather ... well I'd say overbearing. Even Matron didn't stand a chance with him. And I was so ignorant I didn't even know if I *could* leave. And what would I tell Mum? Before I went there I lived at home and worked in the drapers'. There were three quite old ladies working there and the owner was quite an old man, all very straitlaced. So the hospital ... anyway I got this rash up my arms and all over my neck, like red blotches, very itchy, the doctor said it was nerves. It came and went, then came again all the time.'

Despite her timidity Joyce says she managed to avoid going out on excursions or to dances as some of the other nurses did. 'They liked you to go out with the men. Some of the girls enjoyed it. But for me it didn't seem right. It was upsetting that it was expected. You ought to have a choice about those things. I mean you have to do your job—some of it's not very nice, embarrassing at first you know, but fair enough, it's part of the job. But the rest of it ought to be a choice, not expected, and then you got made to feel stupid if you don't want to fool around, that sort of thing. It must sound a bit silly now, these days women are more assertive, and anyway they don't seem to want to say no to anything, they're all ... oh well, you know what I mean.'

Joyce was at East Grinstead for two years, and finally plucked up the courage to move to another hospital where the atmosphere was conventional. She grew to love nursing and qualified as a registered nurse and later as a nursing sister.

'I suppose it toughened me up,' she says, 'but I was glad to get away and the other hospital was quite strict, you knew where you stood and so did the patients. I liked that, because I felt safe. I could even write home and tell Mum about it. I couldn't do that before.'

We talk a little while longer and I sense that Joyce is either tired or holding back so I gather my things together to leave.

'They were wonderfully brave, those men,' she says. 'They suffered terribly, and it wasn't like now, I mean times have changed haven't they? I feel quite bad saying what I have to you because I don't want you to think badly of them. And I did do some things I didn't like and wish I hadn't to try to please them. You can't judge it by how things are today. They were trying to survive and that was their way. Some women had a good time there.'

She gives me the names and addresses of two women who were at East Grinstead at the same time. 'We just send Christmas cards now,' she says. 'I don't know how they'd feel about what I told you.'

*

Back in the studio I turn on my laptop and am able to find a phone number for one of Joyce's contacts. A couple of days later I visit her in Croydon. Bridget Warner was twenty-one when she went to Ward III and had just qualified as a registered nurse. A brisk and rather jolly woman, originally from Dublin, she is now a robust eighty-eight year old. Rather like Moira Nelson, she too had been excited by the prospect of nursing on a plastic surgery ward as a ticket to the future, and she tells me that unlike Joyce she has never been a shrinking violet. She was very forthcoming on the phone but is stiff and a little awkward face to face.

'I didn't mind it,' she tells me when I ask her about McIndoe's unconventional attitude to patients and nurses. 'I loved those boys. Some of the younger girls used to get a bit upset. But they were only boys after all and they'd been through something terrible. I used to tell the girls—you be thankful you're here and not stuck in a burning plane, make allowances but stand up for yourself. It's the least you can do to give that bit extra for them, for the war.

'I was always a bit of a flirt. And they were wonderful boys. So brave, and they stuck together. So what if they were cheeky, and sometimes they played up and it made some extra work? They were always flirting, I'll admit to a few rendezvous in the linen room myself, but it was only fun and you went along with it. Things were different; we were all out for the war and for getting these boys better. I don't know why people make so much of it ... complaining. You did your bit and then a bit more.'

A little later in the conversation Bridget admits that some nurses were intimidated by the Guinea Pigs and by McIndoe's temperament. 'He was very much in charge,' she says. 'You didn't want to argue with him or be caught complaining about the work or the patients. He said exactly what he thought and if you didn't like it you buttoned your lip. He could seem a bit of bully, and Lord Almighty could he shout when something upset him. But if you did your job properly with a smile on your face you had nothing to worry about. He worked so hard, he'd be on his feet in the operating theatre twelve, sometimes sixteen, hours a day. I understood why they called him God, because he would just take on anything. I was always exhausted, and often felt grumpy, but then I'd look at those dear boys going through so much, and Mr McIndoe dead on his feet but still working, and I'd get going again. I was thankful to have escaped from home, particularly from my father and brothers. I knew a bit about men and I'd had a boyfriend. I wanted an adventure and a career and that's what I got. Sometimes they expected too much, but we were all young. What I remember is that those boys loved us. They reckon we saved their lives. That's good enough for me.'

I am just about to start my car when I see Bridget in her doorway beckoning me back. I get out and walk back up the path. 'You shouldn't make too much of this,' she says. 'You mustn't write anything that would upset them or show them in a bad light.'

I ask her if anyone has asked her about this before, or if she has talked about it to family or friends.

'Not really,' she says. 'What's to talk about? It was the war, it was difficult for everyone. It's all in the past.'

I point out that I am not judging the men, who were, after all much the same age as the nurses. It was a different time, with different expectations, but that I think the women's stories are important.

'I can't see it matters that much after all this time,' she says. 'We all had to do things we didn't like for the war. You had to get on with it. You need to remember that.'

13. PAUSE FOR THOUGHT

I found Joyce's story profoundly affecting and had driven home from Canterbury feeling drained. It was not simply what she had told me but the very obvious effect that the telling had on her. She was visibly upset, tense, embarrassed and a couple times on the verge of tears. As I left I'd apologised for upsetting her but she had taken my hand and held on to it very firmly.

'It's a relief to tell someone,' she'd said. 'I went to a reunion at the hospital once and thought I might talk to someone—you know—other nurses, about it. But when I got there I felt ashamed, like when I worked there. As though I had no right to say anything, and it was my fault, for being stupid and well ... prim and prissy.'

Joyce had never told anyone how she felt. She knew that some nurses had fallen in love with patients, had serious relationships and later married them.

'That made me feel more stupid and ashamed, as though there was something wrong with me,' she said. 'But I never told my Mum, I've never even told my husband.'

I asked her what she thought would happen if women did talk openly about this and the effect it had had on them. 'Well they, the men I mean, would be very upset, and they were heroes after all. I think they'd think it was just one silly old woman making a fuss about nothing. I don't think they knew they were doing anything wrong. And it's too long ago. The men just thought it was a joke, there wasn't any real harm in them. I've seen them on the television saying the nurses were wonderful and they saved us and that. But they don't have any idea what it was like for us. I've not forgotten it, I never have.

And I think there'll be others, if they're still alive, that feel the same. You never forget feeling shamed, it taints you, you end up not being able to be yourself, or standing up for yourself without being laughed at—you don't forget that.'

In contrast, after my meeting with Bridget, I felt angry and resentful that she thought it was acceptable for the women's stories to be suppressed. I drove home mumbling furiously to myself and frequently thumping the steering wheel, more determined than ever to pursue the women's experiences.

The following morning it occurs to me that I have become too emotionally involved in Joyce's story because it touches on experiences of my own. As a result I overreacted to both her and Bridget. Perhaps it was also a reaction to that earlier frustration of feeling that I was not going to get below the surface with the Guinea Pigs themselves. I worry that I pressed Joyce too hard and upset her, and offended Bridget, but perhaps I'm overreacting to this too. I realise I need to stand back.

The sun is out and I decide to give myself a day off, take my mind out of the 1940s and 50s, go to the pool for a swim and then relax with some retail therapy. Tomorrow I am meeting Angela and her dissenting uncle. But later, as I get back to the car loaded with carrier bags from a newly discovered boutique, my phone rings. Angela's uncle has a rather nasty cold, she says, they have to postpone the visit to the hospital, can she call me back when he's recovered? I explain that next week I will be in Cornwall—on holiday with my son Mark and daughter-in-law Sarah, who are arriving from Australia, and we are picking up my twin grandsons who live here in the south-west of England with their mother. Angela promises to call me in mid-August to arrange another time to meet. I have a horrible feeling that the uncle has had second thoughts and that the cold is merely an excuse. When the time comes he will actually pull out altogether. I dump my shopping in the boot, flop into the driving seat and close my eyes. Ever since I arrived here I've been up and down to London, often staying overnight to work in the archives and reading rooms. I've driven hundreds of miles to meet people, and sat for hours in snail's pace traffic, frequently in heavy rain, often ending up with no more insight into a situation than I'd had at the start. I've spent whole airless, yawning days in small local libraries, and newspaper archives peering at pages yellowed with age. And I've hovered on street corners eyeing up old people and then accosting them. I probably need that trusty old Bex and a good lie down.

Soon after I get home my phone rings and it's Bridget. She tells me that this morning she phoned her friend Gladys*, to talk to her about our meeting and that Gladys would like to talk to me. So now I have two more contacts: Gladys, and Joyce's other friend, Alice, but I decide to hold back from calling either, aware that I need some distance. Meanwhile, before we set off for Cornwall, I will sit in the sunshine, and read something light and distracting, and nothing to do with the war. But distraction is short-lived. Soon I am back at the keyboard typing up my notes and transcribing the recordings. I need to be sure that I have not put words into Joyce's mouth, nor misinterpreted Bridget's position. And so I stick with it until I have everything down. Then I print it, and the following morning I post the notes and transcripts of our conversation to Joyce, asking her to read it and let me know whether she thinks this is a true record. I apologise again for stirring up the past. Then I do the same with Bridget. And I drop the envelopes in the postbox and set off to meet Mark and Sarah.

*

It's good to have time away from the books, the cuttings, and the notes and transcripts that are piled up on the floor on either side of the small desk in the Hartfield studio. We have rented a house in the heart of Fowey, a small picturesque town typical of many on the Cornish coast: steep, winding streets, where the doors of white-painted cottages open onto the cobbles and window boxes overflow with geraniums and pansies. The house is close to the quay on the banks of the River Fowey. From my bedroom window I can see across the estuary to the village of Bodinnick, where fishing boats bob at anchor and clusters of old cottages and patches of woodland are scattered across the hillside. Fowey was, for many years, the home of one of my favourite writers, the late Daphne du Maurier, an author who was often dismissed as 'too romantic' or 'too concerned with women's things' to be taken seriously by the twentieth-century literary modernists. But, while ignored in literary circles, she was widely published in Britain and overseas and had a huge and devoted readership. It was here that du Maurier wrote several of her much-loved novels and specifically *Rebecca,* which was published in 1938. The initial print run of twenty thousand copies was astoundingly large for the time but within the first month more than twice that number of copies had been sold. *Rebecca* continued to sell in big numbers throughout the war and has never been out of print since then. A little further inland from the town is Menabilly, the house which was the inspiration for Manderley in the novel, and which du Maurier was able to rent and live in for more than twenty years. And from the deck of the ferry that crosses the estuary from Fowey to the nearby port of Mevagissey, you can see the beach that was the setting for the boathouse—the hideaway for Rebecca's romantic trysts. It's great writer country, wild, romantic, beautiful and always slightly haunting.

Despite the pleasures of being with my family in this gorgeous place, I can't get Joyce's story out of my head and I know it is that combination of innocence, ignorance and shame that has disturbed me in a very personal way. Women's lack of information about sex, sexuality and their own bodies is tied to centuries of the ownership of women's sexuality by men, and further disempowerment at the hands of male-dominated organised religion, and the medical and psychiatric professions. In the 1940s both men and women knew a great deal less about sex than they do today when we can all see on television and the internet things that were never spoken of in the comparatively recent past. The Mass Observation diaries of the 1940s revealed that by the end of that decade only eleven per cent of the population had received any sexual education from their mothers, and six per cent from their fathers. Parents were themselves constrained by their own sexual ignorance, and by the prevailing Christian morality that dominated most of society irrespective of individual faith, or the lack of it. The working and middle classes were the most disadvantaged in this respect but the upper classes were little better informed. Most women were virgins when they walked down the aisle wondering what delights or horrors the wedding night had in store for them. There was very little sex education in schools and what information was given to boys was largely confined to the mechanics of sex, while that given to girls was presented in such a way that they were left wondering what it really meant.[47] Despite the fact that Marie Stopes's *Married Love* and *Wise Parenthood* had both been published as early as 1918, information on contraception was still only gradually making its way into the consciousness of young and old alike. Many would have been shocked by the mere idea of buying or being seen reading either these or any other publications on the subject. And nakedness was still taboo in families, especially in front of children. Sex and nudity were considered rude and dangerous.

This attitude continued into the late 1950s and longer in some families, into the early 60s. I was eleven in 1955, and staying with a de facto aunt in London, when I woke one morning to find my sheets stained with blood. I cried out for help and my aunt was landed with the unenviable task of providing a rudimentary explanation of what had happened to me. She gave me some sanitary pads and promised that my mother would explain properly when I got home. In fact my mother was so horrified that she immediately bore me off to a doctor but, too embarrassed to mention this to our elderly and rather gruff family doctor, she made an appointment at another surgery. Her dismay was, she told me years later, largely due to the fact that because she had been almost fifteen when she started menstruating, she was frightened that there was something wrong with me starting so young. The doctor apparently pronounced me to be normal, or at least not abnormal, but I still got no real explanation of what had happened or why. All I learned was that I would have to put up with this once a month for most of my life. A few days later Mum came into my bedroom to say goodnight and gave me a small pink and white striped booklet that the doctor had recommended as suitable reading for me. This, she assured me, would explain everything I needed to know. I've since wondered if she had actually read it. I doubt it. But she would have trusted the reassuring statement on the inside of the cover that it contained 'essential information for young girls'. Sadly that information was so heavily encoded and confusingly explained with examples of tortoises and banana flies (yes really), that I had no idea of what any of it had to do with me and these newly acquired and deeply embarrassing things called periods. I went to a convent which took boys in the junior school, until the 11+ examination, and thereafter only girls. By the time we girls got into the senior school aged twelve we were as ignorant as we had been at the age of five and unlikely to learn anything factual or useful about sex, our own bodies or the male body, from each other or the nuns. Sex is dirty and should be saved for marriage was the confusing message that we were given all through school, and when I left aged sixteen I was no wiser than when I had tried to make sense of the booklet.

Women of Joyce's generation would certainly have had even less information than those of us born in the latter years of the war. I was nineteen before I knew anything about contraception, although I had heard horror stories of abortion, which was seemingly a fate worse than death—and did indeed mean death for many women forced to use backyard abortionists.

In the war years, contraception was rudimentary and unreliable, and access to it was limited. The most frequently practised method was withdrawal. Rubber sheaths were slowly gaining in popularity thanks to improvements in the manufacture of latex. But in the 1940s they were still unpopular with men, and at two or three shillings for a 'packet of three', they made a hole in the wages of a working class man or fumbling boy. The problem with both these methods was that they put contraception in the hands of men, many of whom had no interest in using them. Women had to rely on men to practise withdrawal, or to produce a condom, and would have been considered 'fast' if they bought or carried them themselves.

Early versions of the Dutch cap were available but could only be obtained from a doctor with the consent of a husband, or if a woman was referred to a clinic on gynaecological grounds. Some 'one size fits all' diaphragms could be bought by mail order but were notoriously unreliable and, in any case, for women in poor and cramped living conditions the lack of privacy for inserting or storing a cap was another disadvantage. Many women preferred to use the so-called 'feminine and marriage hygiene' products which were available in chemist shops or by mail order and didn't involve a visit to the doctor. These were douches using spermicides, or small sponges soaked with spermicide and inserted into the vagina. The spermicides came in the form of creams, jellies and foaming tablets, but many were ineffective and some were actually harmful—at least destroying the natural balance of bacteria in the vagina and at worst causing burning or blistering.

Some nurses would have had access to all or any of these, or would have been sufficiently assertive to insist on the use of condoms. But it's likely that most young nurses had no real knowledge about contraception. Even in 1959, when I was fifteen, I knew nothing about sex or contraception except that it involved contact with a penis, but the nature of that contact and the machinery of the penis was a mystery to me. Over the next three years some penis owners introduced me to their own prized possession assuming that I would greet it with enthusiasm, but I was too ignorant and terrified to register anything but dismay. And while I know there were girls of the same age who knew it all, and had perhaps done it all, my level of fear and ignorance was far from unusual. Young men in the early 60s hated using condoms, complained about them and rarely carried them. Many young women faced resistance and resentment from their boyfriends if they either urged or insisted on the use of condoms. What many men did come armed with was the belief (possibly genuine or possibly not) that you couldn't get pregnant if you had sex standing up, or if you practised withdrawal. It was a hazardous situation then and must have been a great deal more hazardous twenty years earlier.

*

During the final few days of our holiday, the impact of Joyce's experience, and the very different stories from Bridget and Moira Nelson, have really got to me. On the way back to Hartfield I more or less decide to abandon the idea of pursuing the nurses. I can still fulfil the requirement of this research trip and it would allow me to restrict myself to McIndoe and the Guinea Pigs. No more looking for or interviewing nurses, no more effort to probe wartime experiences or worry about intrusion, and how that makes them and me feel. And no need to worry about dealing with a subject that could offend the Guinea Pigs themselves. By the time I make it back to Hartfield, I've convinced myself and a great weight has been lifted. Why did I even bother in the first place? The women's role in the whole thing has always been taken for granted. Perhaps Bridget is right—it's all too long ago and I'm not on some sort of crusade. I am just a writer who has appointed herself to the task of uncovering another side of the story.

And then I let myself into the studio and open the mail.

'I can't tell you how much it means to have all this written down so nicely,' Joyce writes. *'I was worried I'd sound silly and I'd be ashamed to read it, but I'm not. I feel quite proud that I was able to talk about it, and people will read it and know what it was like. Although I still couldn't bear it if anyone knew my name.'* In a PS she adds that Bridget will know of course, as will her friend, Alice, and that's all right, but her real name must not be in print in case it upsets the Guinea Pigs.

There is also a letter from Bridget. *'I think I might've been a bit abrupt,'* she writes. *'I know some girls had a hard time of it, mind you some of them lapped it up. But I suppose it should be written down somewhere, and this is all right. I hope you can do it without upsetting anyone, perhaps you don't have to publish it, just store it somewhere. The men might be upset and that wouldn't be right.'*

And there is a postcard from Bridget's friend, Gladys. *'I don't really agree with Bridget, and I would like to meet you. I can tell you what it was like to work at QVH.'*

So much for my new-found sense of relief and release. I wrestle with this for the next few days but now it is with the underlying feeling that having started on this, I have a responsibility to go on. More than anything, it is Joyce's hope that people will 'know what it was like' that finally prompts me back to action. And so a couple of days later I call Gladys who, to my surprise, has a mobile phone. She invites me to meet her in a couple of day's time at a club in London where she's staying. And then there is a call from a journalist on one of the local newspapers whom I met several weeks ago. She sends me a name and address in Dartford for another nurse—Nancy*—whom I call and arrange to meet the day after my meeting with Gladys. Dartford is not far from Bexley Heath where Evelyn lives, and so I arrange to drive to her house, stay the night, and take the train into London.

'I was on the verge of giving up,' I tell Evelyn when I've described my meeting with Joyce and then Bridget.

Evelyn puts a huge mug of tea in front of me and joins me at the kitchen table.

'Well you can't, not now,' she says. 'Just grit your teeth and get on with it. You started it and now you have to finish it.' She then proceeds to take me to task for being a wimp. 'What about you being a feminist and that? You went on and on to me about women's stories not being told, so what was all that about? Now you want to give up when you only just started. I can't make any sense of you, you are totally strong and fearless about so many things, but you're like a jelly about this.'

She's right about the latter, but I am *never* fearless. I am always in a state of fear. The intensity of it varies but it's always part of who I am. I have, however, always been successful in hiding it. My body is always tense, my mind roaming—searching out danger where it doesn't exist, expecting that something terrible is about to happen. I jump at loud noises, lie awake at night agonising over what should really be only minor concerns, catastrophise the smallest problems, fear not being good enough at anything. I dream of being crushed and smothered by crumbling walls and ceilings that cave in. I imagine being shamed for something stupid I've done, or accused of something I haven't done, being abandoned by my family and friends. The idea of admitting this to Evelyn is itself terrifying. And so I say nothing.

'It just sounds like a load of excuses to me,' she says. And we launch into a long and quite disturbing conversation in which she gets me to admit that, despite my feminist activism, I am still easily intimidated by the prospect of male disapproval, especially the disapproval of men I like, admire or love, and certainly men in authority.

'Good lord,' she says. 'You're telling me that some of these women have kept quiet to protect the men's feelings? And now you want to protect them too. It doesn't make sense. *You* don't make sense.'

And of course she's right.

14. UNREASONABLE DEMANDS

Gladys's club is in an elegant Victorian building in Kensington. Stepping inside it like stepping back at least a century. 'It's a bit of an anachronism,' Gladys says when I admire the elegant surroundings. 'Women's clubs, men's clubs—almost a thing of the past.' This club is for retired business and professional women, and she tells me she regularly spends two or three weeks, even a month, staying here. The rest of the time she lives with her sister and brother-in-law in Tunbridge Wells. 'It's good for me to get away,' Gladys explains. 'They're even older than me.'

She is a tall woman, slightly stooped, but she moves surprisingly quickly with the support of a stick. I assume she is in her mid-eighties, so I'm taken aback when she tells me she is ninety-two. We settle in the lounge and Gladys orders tea, which is delivered along with tiny cucumber sandwiches and rock cakes. She gives me a conspiratorial grin. 'This is part of the reason I come here. It makes me feel like a grand old lady.'

Gladys was twenty-six and nursing in a London hospital when she was spotted by Archibald McIndoe. 'He'd been asked to look at a young pilot who was badly burned and I was nursing him. Mr McIndoe decided to move him to East Grinstead and he said to me, "You should come too, nurse, I've heard what a good job you're doing". I was quite good looking then,' she smiles, putting her hand up to her hair. She is still a good-looking woman with a strong presence despite her slow speech and the fact that she frequently stops for breath. 'My hair may be grey now but then it was red and it had a natural curl. A lot of my friends envied it. I was tall and had a nice figure. I was taller than Mr McIndoe. He was a bit intimidating, so I was glad of my height! Well, cut a long story short, three weeks later I was off to East Grinstead, and put up in one of the houses that had been set up for the nurses.'

Gladys had seen many severe injuries from the war but it hadn't prepared her for what she saw at East Grinstead. 'Perhaps because there were so many, and they were the worst possible cases,' she says. 'There was no one there with anything normal like pneumonia or an appendix or even minor burns. And I remember it being crowded with things you didn't see in a normal ward: the beer barrel, a piano, the saline baths. It was hot and airless and it all seemed very intense.'

After the strict discipline of a top London hospital, the casual atmosphere, the behaviour of the patients, and the challenges that presented to nurses also took Gladys by surprise. 'Straight away—that first day—the patients were calling me Ginger. No patient had ever called me anything except Nurse, before, and if they had done the sister would have put a stop to it. Nursing training was very strict in those days, and part of it was you were told not to get familiar with the patients. Discipline was the first thing you were supposed to learn and that was also about making sure patients didn't cross the line with you, and keeping the ward quiet and orderly. But it was all first names at East Grinstead, and jokes, and saucy comments. And the same day a man with a burned face and hands rode into the ward on one of those old black bikes with a basket on the front, like we had then, a woman's bike. Well he parked the bike in the middle of the ward—how he rode it with those stumps of hands I'll never know. Anyway, he'd got a paper bag in the basket and he was holding it in his two stumps, and he started calling out, "Eccles cakes anyone?" And another man with a lot of bandages on his head came up and grabbed the bag and started throwing the cakes onto the beds. "One for you, one for you ..." I wondered where I'd ended up.'

For a couple of weeks Gladys was on the brink of leaving because she found Ward III so confronting. 'What made me stay was seeing how Mr McIndoe loved those boys, and the lengths he'd go to for them. And he was so determined to get them back to work or back into the RAF. I thought it was important, and the men ... well a lot of them were lovely and so brave, that was the other thing, I didn't want to give up on them, even though they were difficult and really out of line. I didn't like the way the nurses were treated and a lot of the sexy stuff that went on. I ... well I was going to say there was no respect for us but that's not really right. I think they did respect us, and they knew they were dependent on us in a lot of things, but they knew more or less they could do as they liked. I wasn't happy with that. But what do you do? It was the opposite of what we were taught, but it was what Mr McIndoe wanted, and Matron wasn't able to do anything about it. I never said anything. I wasn't very assertive in those days. I was lucky; being tall made a difference. They were a bit more cautious with me than some of the others. They didn't mean any harm but ... oh you see ... they took liberties and they didn't think about how we felt. If you looked a bit po-faced they ribbed you something shocking. You could have a nice chat with one on his own, but when they got going as a group they behaved badly. If Matron Hall spoke up, Mr McIndoe could be quite rude to her. The men were all that mattered. The other girls used to say, "Oh well they're war heroes, we have to do our bit." Well it was demeaning and it wasn't what I signed up for when I became a nurse. So I suppose I was a feminist even then.'

Gladys stayed at East Grinstead for almost two years, and left in 1942 when she got engaged to a man who worked at the BBC, whom she'd met in hospital before the war. He was almost ten years older than her and she had been a trainee nurse when he arrived on her ward.

'He'd been going to work on the bus and he jumped off from the running board before the bus stopped and he fell and a car ran into him. He lost a leg and had quite a lot of other injuries. So he wasn't called up,' she explains. 'We were very happy, me and my lovely Frank, but he wasn't very strong because of that accident. I lost him in nineteen ninety-eight, he was the love of my life, there was never anyone else for me, before or after. He didn't want me to go to East Grinstead but I said, well it's my job and I want to give it a go, so he didn't stand in my way. He'd come down on the train sometimes and stay in the town for a couple of nights, but it was hard to meet because the hours were very long, and I was always worn out. That's why I left in the end, because we decided to get married. Frank took his time asking me though.' Gladys laughs out loud remembering this, loud enough for some women at another table to look up in surprise. 'Said he didn't like to because he was so much older and that and his leg and everything might make him a liability. But he never was.'

Gladys occasionally went with patients to dances or sometimes down to Brighton. 'I didn't mind doing that but I didn't like them crossing the lines if you know what I mean.'

I asked her to explain. 'Well if you go out with a man whose hands are burned to stumps you had to do things for him. Like you cut up his food, maybe you have to feed him. You have to feel in his pockets for money to pay, and then you'd put the money on his stump for him so he could hand it to the waitress. You have to help him with his coat or his jacket ... and well ... if there wasn't another man around to help you'd have to go to the gentlemen's lavatory and undo his buttons, and you might have to ... well hold it for him. Now, you can do all those things as a nurse, you do very personal ... intimate things for them every day because it's part of your job. But if you cross the line and go out with them on a date then those things might seem like something different. That's when the lines get crossed and they can think it's something different from just what you do in your job.'

Gladys overcame this by only ever going out with a group, and sticking firmly to her own idea of herself as a nurse on duty. So she might end up doing the awkward things for more than one man, 'And I'd be very brisk about it, no nonsense you know. I'd take two or three of them to the lavatory so it was more impersonal. And I could do that because I'd been trained and I'd had some experience. I was older. Some of the young girls got caught up in crossing lines, and ended up in difficulties back at work because they couldn't keep the men at a distance. That was unfair on them I think.'

Gladys stops talking, closes her eyes and rests her head on the back of her chair. I look at my watch and see that we've been talking and drinking tea for some time and she's probably exhausted. I begin to gather my things together and she opens her eyes and sits up straight.

'You don't have to go,' she says, but I can see she's being polite. I thank her and tell her I need to catch a train. 'I'd like to talk to you again,' she says, 'if you have time.'

I promise I'll call soon to make a time. 'What you said about crossing the lines—the boundaries, has been really helpful,' I tell her.

'Boundaries,' she says, 'that was the word I wanted—boundaries. He—Mr McIndoe—dissolved them all, that was the problem, and so some women were coerced into things they didn't want to do. But it was probably what saved those young men's lives, made them want to live. It's an interesting moral dilemma isn't it?' And she grins mischievously. 'We can get our teeth into that one next time.'

In the 1950s Gladys decided that she was done with nursing and wanted to train as a doctor, and with some persistence on her own and her husband's part she was eventually admitted to medical school, qualifying in the 60s. It was, she said, being at East Grinstead that made her want to be a doctor. 'I felt that if there had been a woman doctor on the staff it might have helped the patients and the nurses. And if there were two or three women it would have been even better.'

'She's probably right!' Evelyn says when, back at her house that evening, I tell her what Gladys has said. 'Unless they turned out to be intimidated by the men.' And she gives me a big grin and opens a bottle of gin.

*

The following morning I drive to Dartford in pouring rain and find my way to the address the East Grinstead journalist gave me. I am met at the door by a man who tells me his name is Stan and he is Nancy's second husband; she has just popped next door to take some soup to a neighbour who has had a fall.

'Always helping someone,' he says, offering me a cup of tea. 'She's never stopped being a nurse.' And he goes on tell me that Nancy was at East Grinstead for a short time in 1943, and that her first husband was a patient there.

'One of the burns patients?' I ask.

'That's it,' he says, 'badly burned.'

Nancy though, is less forthcoming about her late, first husband. 'Yes he was one of them,' she says, 'but no, I won't tell you his name because you might write it. He was burned but not as bad as some of the others. He went back into the RAF when he'd been fixed up at East Grinstead. He was flying again then.'

This conversation is difficult. I have the feeling that Nancy wishes she hadn't agreed to see me, and she certainly skirts around her experience and talks at some length about the Guinea Pigs and McIndoe's regime. But there is nothing I haven't already heard from others. And she's reluctant to talk about her own feelings.

I move on to the subject of the relationships between the nurses and the patients.

'You got very close to them because you thought you might be dead tomorrow,' she says. 'You saw them every day and you did things for them that no one had done before, things they used to be able to do for themselves. You wanted to make them happy and do something for the war and you felt proud when you did. So you fitted in even if it went against what you thought was right.'

'Was that fair to the nurses?' I ask. And there is quite a long silence.

'No, it wasn't. But you don't have to make a big thing of it, do you? I don't want them to think I've said something unkind about them. And I'm not saying anymore. Nobody was forced to do anything they didn't want to do.'

It's clear from Nancy's expression that she is very uncomfortable, but also quite determined. We talk about less contentious subjects and then the Guinea Pig whom she would later marry and who was almost at the end of his treatment when they met. She had stayed on at the hospital when he went back to the RAF. They weren't in touch for some time after that, but met up again a year or so after the war ended and another year later they were married. 'He didn't go back there, only once for a check up. He didn't get much involved in the club.'

'Why was that?' I ask.

Nancy shrugs. 'He wasn't that sort of person. He was more individual, a loner, always very sure of himself. He liked it that people saw his injuries and thought he was a hero, although he wasn't on duty when it happened. He'd come off-duty and was at a party in London and the house was bombed. Mr McIndoe saw him in the hospital and took him to the Queen Vic and fixed him up. Then he went back into the RAF, that was what he wanted.'

The atmosphere is increasingly chilly and I make moves to leave, shaking hands with Stan who goes through to the back of the house. Nancy follows me to the front door.

'One thing,' she says, as I'm about to leave, 'he didn't do us any favours.'

I stop and turn back. 'Your husband?'

'Mr McIndoe. He didn't do the women any favours. He told the men they were heroes and that meant they could have whatever they wanted. He was always after women, my husband, he thought that was his due. Unfaithful to me all his life he was. Two women he had affairs with turned up at his funeral. No, whatever he did for the men he didn't do us any favours.'

Driving back to Evelyn's house I try to figure out why Nancy even agreed to see me. It's clear she was very uncomfortable and, I think, resentful about speaking to me. Did she get cold feet? Was it the very genial Stan who persuaded her? Or did she just need to get that last bit of bile off her chest to someone?

'Of course, it might be nothing to do with being at East Grinstead,' Evelyn says later. 'Her husband might just have been a man who was congenitally unfaithful.'

Of course he might. On the other hand he might not.

15. THE BOSS

It's evident from biographies and memoirs, and from Emily Mayhew's definitive history, that Archibald McIndoe was a towering figure at East Grinstead. A difficult, often irascible and intimidating man, it was he who sanctioned the schoolboy pranks, the disruptive behaviour and the heightened sexual tension in Ward III. While he certainly did pull men into line over bad behaviour it was not, as far as I could discover, ever in relation to flirting, sexual activity or relationships with nurses. He was, however, concerned that his work in getting the townspeople and the wider community to accept the Guinea Pigs, was not undermined by their behaviour, and he came down on them over misdemeanours beyond hospital grounds.

Jim Fitzgerald, who grew up in East Grinstead some years ahead of me and who now lives in New Zealand, wrote to me about his memory of that time. His father, Joe, was a driver whose job was to drive the nurses and medical staff to and from work, and to ferry the Guinea Pigs back and forth to parties and other dances at some of the big houses in the area. He also drove the men to and from Marchwood Park, an RAF convalescent home and retraining centre for injured and disabled aircrew near Hythe, in Hampshire which, he says, was the scene of some riotous parties.

> I remember one of the parties resulted in a bunch of the boys stealing the bus they used and getting it jammed between two trees. My dad got the blame for letting it happen but no action was taken. The GPs were only young guys, and as soon as they started to recover they wanted

> to party, after their experiences they had no inhibitions about riotous behaviour they were a bit of a handful at times, my Dad was ex-army, a big strong Irishman and he could handle them well it would seem.[48]

If Jim is correct and his father got the blame, it may perhaps have been that Jim's father generously took the fall for the men, because other similar 'pranks' at Marchwood Park brought the wrath of their personal god down on the men responsible. Mosley records that in September 1943 McIndoe received a complaint from the Air Ministry about the behaviour of four Guinea Pigs who had been staying at the centre. This, he says, was the second example of misdemeanours there, the previous one involving a bus. On this second occasion the riotous behaviour and noisy return from the pub of four men in the wee small hours had severely upset the staff at Marchwood Park, who had put the drunken men to bed. The Wing Commander in charge felt that this particular occasion and others on which they had returned late, drunk and noisy, could lead to a scandal. McIndoe was furious and sent Edward Blacksell to Marchwood to check out the reports and apologise. The four men were then returned to East Grinstead and McIndoe delivered a half-hour tirade to all the service patients winding up with a threat of severe punishments in future. He later wrote to the Air Ministry with a personal apology explaining that the rules at East Grinstead were that the men must be home by 10 pm on weekdays, with passes until 11 pm only occasionally allowed. On weekends the time was 10.30 pm with concessions until 12.30 if there was a dance. A first offence, he claimed, would result in the offenders being relegated to wearing hospital blues. Second offences would see them sent to their commanding officer for action to be taken.[49]

McIndoe's letter implies that this action was taken in every case of a breach of the rules, but the anecdotal evidence of Guinea Pigs themselves, nurses and other hospital staff, is that the curfews were regularly broken, and it was common for men to return in the early hours very much the worse for wear, disturbing other patients and having to be calmed down, sobered up or just put to bed by the nurses who did not report their behaviour. It was when that behaviour drew complaints from outsiders that McIndoe reacted strongly. On one occasion when a borrowed car was crashed into a local resident's fence, and another when damage was caused by bad behaviour in an out-of-town pub, McIndoe sent Edward Blacksell to visit the residents and the publican, to apologise and arrange the immediate payment of compensation. The men responsible were confined to their hospital blues as punishment. He reacted strongly to anything he saw as a breach of that relationship of trust and understanding that he had with his patients, especially if it had the potential to bring disgrace on the Guinea Pigs and hospital. The men themselves, however, were consistently uncritical of his style of management in the ward or of the man himself, and he is still spoken of with enormous admiration and affection. As Emily Mayhew points out he is indeed often portrayed by them as 'close to saintly—an inaccurate and unhelpful characterisation'. She adds:

> McIndoe the man was no saint; he was consumed by his work as a surgeon, sacrificing much of his personal life, including his marriage and the health of his first wife, to this obsessive devotion to his patients and their care. There was a fine line between being forthright and being a bully and McIndoe frequently crossed it. He could and did crush his own staff, his patients and their families, even his own friends and family usually with no regard or apology for the consequences.[50]

Sebastian Faulks, in his short biography of Richard Hillary goes further:

> [McIndoe] was ambitious, bullying, mean and crafty. He had charm but used it only when his

> natural aggression had not won him his way. He had compassion, vision and generosity of heart but they were not qualities he found it necessary to keep on display. He had one further ability: he could give his patients hope. They came to believe that, whatever his shortcomings, he was a great man.[51]

McIndoe was also held in the highest esteem by the local community. Most locals were somewhat in awe of him due to his authoritative manner and his assumption that people would do as he asked. He made a point of forming acquaintances and friendships in the area, especially with some of the wealthier families, many of whom owned large estates. John and Kathleen Dewar of the Dewar's whisky family were typical of these. They had already endowed the Dewar Ward at East Grinstead, which was reserved for women, and had turned over the main part of their home, Dutton Homestall, as a convalescent home. Here, as at Saint Hill Manor, the property leased by Elaine and Neville Blond, the men were treated like members of an extended family and social and entertainment events were organised for them. Frequently their hosts arranged female company for their convalescent service guests, inviting the single daughters of their friends to come along to talk and dance with them. Betty Parrish, who lived in the nearby village of Lingfield at the time, told me that she had packed her bags and left home in fury the day that her mother had told her that, for the third time, she had volunteered her as a date on a Guinea Pig outing.

'I didn't mind the men themselves,' she told me. 'But I really objected to being farmed out to flirt with them, or whatever else they might have in mind.'

Interestingly, despite the support of these and so many women of all classes in the local community, McIndoe had no compunction in moving the women patients out of the Dewar Ward and moving 'his boys' in there when a streptococcal infection created havoc in Ward III. Matron

Hall received an abrupt order to get the women out, wash down the men with antiseptic and move them in. 'When Matron Hall hesitated, he said: "And get on with it, woman." Matron Hall went instead to the resident doctors who, in turn, confronted McIndoe, but he would not be moved. The women were transferred to other wards and some were sent home.[52]

It is doubtful that a lesser, more accommodating man could have achieved what McIndoe achieved in the hospital, the town, and most of all in the hearts and minds of his patients. And it was predominantly men whom he treated. Despite his pre-war reputation for facial cosmetic surgery, which had brought him female clients from the world of entertainment and high society, he appears to have chosen not to work on women during the war. From time to time a female patient would be sent to him by a surgeon from another hospital, but I could find no evidence of his selecting a burned WAAF, or any other burned woman, in his rounds of other hospitals and moving her to East Grinstead. Despite the ban on women flying in combat, many did fly during the war, particularly the women of the Air Transport Auxilliary who came to England from a variety of countries around the world to undertake work that was almost as dangerous. The women pilots of the ATA delivered Spitfires, Hurricanes and Lancasters to RAF bases, from where they were flown into combat by male pilots. These women flew unarmed and without radios or instruments, always at risk of long-range enemy aircraft and hazardous weather. Many were injured and some badly burned in the course of their work, and fifteen, including flying pioneer Amy Johnson, were killed.[53] Similarly, many WAAFs were burned in aircraft or airfield crashes and fires, and elsewhere on the home front.

I found only two links to McIndoe operating on service women but there were no details attached. Civilian women were treated for burns at East Grinstead during the war, but whether they were treated by McIndoe or Percy Jayes, the resident surgeon, or one of the many young plastic surgeons whom McIndoe trained in his time there, is not clear. Margaret Chadd, the almoner whose recollections are posted on the BBC Archive, *The People's War*, records her memories of four women treated there.

One, whom she calls Joan, was an eighteen year old who worked in a London sweet factory, and was mixing toffee when the factory was bombed and she was covered from head to foot in boiling sugar. When she arrived some time later at East Grinstead, having first been treated in London, she was also suffering from bedsores. Her hair, still coated with toffee, stuck out in sticks and was seething with maggots, and her bones protruded through her charred flesh. Chadd also recalls Maisie, nineteen, who was bombed two days before her wedding day, and arrived at East Grinstead with tiny fragments of broken glass embedded all over her face. And Gladys, who was dancing with her fiancé at the Café de Paris the night it was bombed, suffered similar severe facial damage, and her whole body was impregnated with tiny pieces of glass. Rose, a munitions worker during the war but a dressmaker by trade, had both her hands blown off at the wrists in an air raid.[54] All these women underwent many operations at East Grinstead over a period of years.

Emily Mayhew points out that Archibald McIndoe's prime concern was to restore function to his male patients. He wanted to get them back to active service or other suitable civilian employment, and to be able to hold their own in a world that would greet them with shock and distaste. I wondered whether, as a man who believed that it was essentially women's function to be beautiful and available to men, McIndoe may have avoided working on them because he knew he could not restore that function. After all, it is widely recorded that his reconstructive work on the Guinea Pigs was primarily on restoration of function rather than attempting to recapture any pre-war good looks. I put this possibility to both Emily Mayhew and McIndoe's daughter, Vanora Marland. Both said that this was possible and Vanora added that she felt it quite likely. It is, however, simply my own observation based on what I've learned about his attitude to women.

Whatever empathy and consideration McIndoe lacked in dealing with his staff, he frequently made up for with occasional acts of great kindness and thoughtfulness if staff were in trouble. But it was the exclusive and unique relationship with the patients that took priority over everything else. Every boss, however, needs a strong team and McIndoe had picked the best. His initial team of assistant surgeon Percy Jayes, theatre sister Jill Mullins and anaesthetist John Hunter were with him from day one, as was William Kelsey Fry (later Sir William) who was establishing a dental and jaw unit that was essential to the maxillo-facial work. By 1941 two more RAF surgeons had been appointed to the hospital, together with a second anaesthetist, Russell Davis. By 1941, the burns victims treated at East Grinstead included many men from the Royal Canadian Air Force, and the principal medical officer of the RCAF (Overseas) was also despatched to East Grinstead on a permanent posting. Ross Tilley had been trained by plastic surgeons in Canada and spent his first few months polishing his skills alongside McIndoe.[55] The two men developed a warm and respectful working relationship and Tilley soon became the friend and colleague on whom McIndoe relied to discuss and experiment with new and different ways of developing the work in the Burns Unit. Tilley went on to develop a Canadian surgical team at the hospital, and was later instrumental in persuading the Canadian Government to fund the building of a Canadian Wing. The foundation stone was laid in December 1943 and in July 1944 the first nine patients were admitted to the new wing. More staff were added to McIndoe's team through his assiduous training of young and enthusiastic surgeons wishing to learn his techniques in plastic surgery. Many of these moved on to other RAF hospitals and others soon filled their places.

Matron Hall bore the brunt of much of the surgeon's erratic and autocratic behaviour. Margaret Chadd describes Caroline Hall, as 'a warm, loveable and approachable Irish lady of middle age, who tried hard to keep a firm hand on the "lads".'[56] Under her direct authority were the nursing sisters: her own sister, Cherry Hall, Mary Meally and Sister Harrington. Jill Mullins and Sister Walker were responsible for managing the operating theatres, and were later joined by Sister Dorothy Wagstaff. Very little is recorded about the nursing staff as individuals, often not even their first names, but Hugh McLeave writes that Sister Mary Meally, who ran Ward III for several years, 'acted, in her quiet Irish way, as a matchmaker, and, in fact, married one of the patients.'[57] Sister Meally's was one of several marriages between nurses or other hospital staff and Ward III patients. Among them were Canadian flyer Holebrook Mahn, who came to East Grinstead after fourteen days at sea in a rubber dinghy suffering from immersion frostbite, similar to Alan Morgan. Hoke, as he was known on Ward III, eventually married Betty Andrews, a WAAF orderly who assisted with the saline baths, and Bill Foxley married Catherine Arkell.

Above all, McIndoe relied on Jill Mullins both in the operating theatre and in his personal life. They had met first in 1931 when she was a theatre nurse at St Bartholomew's Hospital in London. He spotted her first as a fine nurse and enjoyed her witty company, and he soon came to rely on her in the operating theatre. She went on to work with him at the London Clinic and the Hospital for Tropical Medicine, before moving to East Grinstead. Mullins was popular with the staff and with the Guinea Pigs. A tall attractive woman with red-gold hair and green eyes, she had a great sense of humour and a strong personality that enabled her to manage wayward Guinea Pigs with confidence. She was by then in her early to mid-thirties. In 1941 she began a relationship with a patient, Flying Officer Geoffrey Page, who had been shot down in the English Channel the previous year. They were together for two years before coming to a mutual decision to end the relationship because, according to Page, 'the spark had gone out'.[58]

Adonia McIndoe was still in America, and Jill Mullins and McIndoe grew closer in their working and personal relationship. He relied on her in the operating theatre where she anticipated his needs and frequently finished his procedures. Outside the hospital she regularly accompanied him to social events, and often stayed with him at Little Warren, where she also acted as hostess for dinners and drinks with selected Guinea Pigs. Adonia insisted on returning to England with their daughters in 1943, but by that time the McIndoe marriage had deteriorated beyond repair.

Hugh McLeave describes an episode that seems to have become the stuff of Ward III folklore, as Guinea Pigs and a couple of nurses repeated it to me. One night a fellow doctor got a late call from McIndoe to come to his aid at the cottage. Jill, he said, had tripped and fallen, hitting her face on a table and he needed to patch up her nose. She had in fact broken her nose on the bedside table, and was bleeding heavily. The doctor persuaded McIndoe that it was too serious to deal with at the cottage and an anaesthetist and another nurse were woken with instructions to turn up without delay at the hospital. Jill Mullins's nose was repaired in a theatre in the Canadian Wing but was left scarred. Some time later McIndoe operated again and she acquired the retroussé McIndoe nose which he had perfected before the war and which, a decade later, he provided for film star Kay Kendall, and for Dame Margot Fonteyn.[59]

It was Jill Mullins who had been at Archibald McIndoe's side in the theatre, and was with him in 1943, when he underwent exploratory surgery for cancer. This proved to be just a problem with the appendix, which was removed. And she was with him again three weeks later when he collapsed in acute pain and underwent a second operation which revealed that the surgeon had left a four-inch swab inside him. In difficult times she had often confided to friends and colleagues that she expected to become the next Mrs McIndoe, and the man himself made no attempt to deny the rumours. The McIndoes separated in 1946 and the following year he was awarded a knighthood for his wartime work. Jill Mullins had been living with him at Little Warren for some time, and he later bought her a cottage of her own. Mosley suggests that despite their closeness at this time McIndoe never had any thought of marrying Jill Mullins, despite the fact that both his daughters would have welcomed this.[60] In 1950, however, he introduced her to his mother as the woman he intended to marry, but it was 1953 before the McIndoe divorce was finalised on the grounds of his adultery, confirmed by photographs taken in a hotel with a woman whom he had paid to cooperate. It was a common practice in those days, and the only way for a couple whose relationship had become impossible, to end a marriage.

McIndoe's two biographers differ in a number of areas and one is in their accounts of the events that followed the divorce. McLeave writes that at about the time the decree absolute was granted, Jill Mullins had an uneasy feeling that she might have a rival, but decided to stay silent and did not confide her fears to anyone. One morning as she walked to work at the London Clinic she passed a newsstand and saw, on the front page of the newspaper, the announcement that Sir Archibald McIndoe was to marry Mrs Constance Belchem. Connie Belchem was a divorcee whom Jill and Archie had met on holiday some years earlier in the South of France. Jill was devastated at the news of the engagement and was supported by friends through this crisis. An icy silence existed between her and McIndoe as they worked alongside each other from that time onwards. McIndoe and Connie Belchem married the following year and some time later Jill Mullins left nursing to marry a South African businessman and moved with him to Johannesburg.[61] Mosley's version differs in that he contextualises this as a time when women were closing in on McIndoe. His daughter Vanora accused him in a letter of being 'a terrible cynic about women ... are we always quite so awful as we seem when you sound off about us?'[62] His mother was urging him to reunite with Adonia, and Mosley adds that if there had ever been a moment when he would have thought of marrying Jill Mullins that moment had passed. Jill, he suggests, was well aware that Constance Belchem was the woman in McIndoe's life and he never concealed that fact from her. When Connie arrived in England in 1952 announcing that she was divorcing her husband, Archie immediately set proceedings in motion for his own divorce, and asked her to marry him, but they kept the necessary distance from each other until the McIndoe divorce was granted in 1953, and the Belchems' in 1954. When the engagement was announced it was, Mosley suggests 'not so much a surprise or a blow to Jill Mullins as the confirmation of her worst fear, and she reacted badly at first to the news.'[63] He adds that the two women eventually formed a friendship of mutual respect. It is perhaps worth mentioning here that McLeave's biography was published in 1961, the year after McIndoe's death, and Leonard Mosley's was promptly commissioned by his widow who retained powers of veto over the final text, and this second biography was published in 1962.

Holidaying back in England in 1959, Jill Mullins visited the McIndoes before heading home by ship. On the journey she suffered a stroke. A call was made to McIndoe at the London Clinic and arrangements were made to fly her there. But before that could happen she suffered a second stroke and died. Jill Mullins was buried at sea a few days later. She was just forty-nine. McIndoe is said to have been devastated for weeks. He wrote a touching memorial to her and arranged for a new nurses home to be built at East Grinstead and to be named after her.

Why, after so many years of a relationship that embraced his professional and personal life so fully, Archibald McIndoe might have chosen to let Jill Mullins find out about his engagement through a newspaper, no one seems to know. But it is one more piece of information that can perhaps tell us more about the man himself and how he saw the role of women in his life and work.

16. THE OUTSIDER

I have given up on the hope of talking to Angela's dissenting uncle but, good as her word, she calls again at the end of August, and on a warm Friday afternoon I set out to meet them at the hospital café, with no idea of what to expect. I wander back and forth along the paved path that leads to the café, the path along which patients were wheeled to the operating theatre, and spot Angela in the car park, pulling a wheelchair from the back of a car, with the help of an elderly man. She introduces me to the man whose name is Dennis and who goes around the car to extract the other passenger.

'My uncle has multiple sclerosis,' she tells me, 'it's ups and downs as you probably know. But he's pretty good today.' And shortly Dennis wheels him out from between the cars, and Arthur*, Angela's uncle, introduces himself.

'Sorry, not much grip,' he says with a wry grin as he extends a shaking hand.

We head back to the café and I order tea and scones and bring them to the table. It's pleasantly quiet in here this afternoon. That's a blessing as Arthur's voice is soft and distorted by his illness.

'I haven't been back here for decades,' he tells me. 'Haven't wanted to, although I did come near here to visit a friend in Copthorne, at the Cheshire Home—place called Heatherley, a few miles from here. It's near a pub called The Hedgehog.'

I tell him that I know The Hedgehog well and was there recently with Guinea Pigs, and that I also know Heatherley, because my father was one of the people involved in starting the home. Arthur tells me that the friend he visited there was Squadron Leader 'Ginger' Farrell DFC, a World War II pilot who, like Arthur himself, contracted multiple sclerosis after the war. 'His wife really got it going,' he continues. 'Pamela, she was a bit of a legend. I came to the opening of that home, and a few years later to see Ginger.'

This is spooky—I feel the goosebumps on my arms. Pam and Ginger Farrell were close friends of my parents, and it was through them that my father became a member of the board of management of Heatherly. Cheshire Homes, which now care for a variety of people with disabilities, were established by Group Captain Leonard Cheshire (later Lord Cheshire) and his wife Sue Ryder. Cheshire was the only man awarded a Victoria Cross for consistent acts of bravery during World War II. Later, he and Sue Ryder established 270 homes for the disabled and dying around the world. After the war Ginger Farrell qualified in medicine, was a house-surgeon at Guy's Hospital in London and later moved into general practice in Copthorne, a village that lies roughly between East Grinstead and Crawley—and is where I lived as a child. It was around this time that he developed multiple sclerosis. Pam Farrell was, indeed, a legend and she spearheaded the purchase of Heatherley, a large old country house with several acres of land there as part of the Cheshire Foundation. Heatherley was opened in 1961. Ginger later became a patient and died there in November 1966 at the age of just forty-four.

'I knew Pam and Ginger and their two sons, and I was at the opening of Heatherley,' I say and Arthur and I stare at each other, shaken by this coincidence. Soon we are holding hands across the table wondering if we ever actually met or, as seems more likely, if he might have met my parents. It's an emotional moment for both of us, and the extraordinary circumstance of my having sat at Angela's table in the Victoria Station café makes it seem as though this meeting was meant to be. Eventually Angela suggests that she and Dennis will leave Arthur and me here to talk, while they drive to Sainsbury's for some shopping.

'So how does it feel, to be back here?' I ask once we are alone.

Arthur shrugs and looks around. 'A mite odd. But impersonal, it doesn't seem like the same place.' He goes on to tell me a little about the circumstances that brought him here in 1943, when he was just twenty-one. He was flying a Hurricane when he was hit by enemy fire, and started to limp back across the Channel, but as he approached the Kent coast, the fuel tank burst into flames. Arthur attempted to escape but had difficulty releasing his parachute. By the time he broke free the flames had reached him. He bailed out and landed on the beach near Hythe, and was delivered to East Grinstead a couple of days later.

'I was luckier than most,' he told me. 'As you can see, only one side of my face was burned, as well as my ear, neck and shoulder, my arm and hand. McIndoe managed to save a couple of my fingers, which has been a godsend. The arm works and the fingers work pretty well—or did before the MS got me, and he fixed up my ear and face. Bloody miracle really. It took several operations, but my parents lived in Lewes, so I was able to spend a lot of time at home.'

After the war Arthur returned to university to finish his degree, and later a PhD, and he has lectured in history at universities in England and Canada. He developed MS in the late 60s, around the last time he saw Ginger Farrell, but for a time it progressed only very slowly.

'And you don't think of yourself as a Guinea Pig?' I ask eventually.

'Well I was, obviously, one of McIndoe's guinea pigs, by default—we all were. But I extracted myself from the whole idea of the Guinea Pig Club. Not that there was anything wrong with it. It's been a wonderful thing for those that wanted to be part of it.'

I pour him another cup of tea and wait in silence hoping he'll go on, but he doesn't.

'Angela says you are a dissenter,' I prompt.

He nods. 'I have used that word but it might give a wrong impression. It's not that I didn't agree with it, it just wasn't right for me. I wasn't comfortable. Sure, it was a men's club, which often has an appeal for chaps of my persuasion. But I was very much in the closet in those days, and I was afraid of being "outed" as they say these days.'

This actually blindsides me; as I had wracked my brains for possible causes of dissent, this had not been among them.

'I should probably just call myself an "outsider",' Arthur adds. 'That makes more sense. But if you've talked to other people, and read what it was like here, you'd understand that it was a difficult place to be for a man like me. I was young, inexperienced and scared stiff, so I just kept my head down and tried to pretend I was the same as everyone else. But I had nightmares about being dragged out of bed in the ward and crouching on the floor surrounded by men shouting "queer", "pervert", "pansy", "faggot" and some other names I won't repeat. Probably that sounds pathetic but that's how it was. It was how I felt—pathetic, I mean.'

I ask Arthur what he thinks would really have happened if someone *had* found out.

He smiles and gives a little shrug. 'Well I don't know really, it was just the fear, an encompassing sort of fear of shame, abuse perhaps, being on the sharp end of that very macho culture. I was afraid of physical violence, you heard about it a lot in those days. Boys getting roughed up in back streets, murdered even. And of course the police, they were as homophobic as you could get. Homosexuality was illegal and the penalties were pretty hideous. But these days I feel differently. I mean I remember the fear, but they were a good bunch. We'd all been through hell and most of them were a lot worse off than me. I like to think that sort of experience makes people more generous and forgiving, but who knows. You often only need one or two bigots or bullies to turn a group and I wasn't taking any chances. But at the same time there wasn't one man in there that I feared or who was ever hostile to me personally. But all I wanted was to get away as soon as I could and to stop pretending I was someone else. So I was lucky to have my parents not so far away, and go home a lot. The club wasn't for me.'

We talk on about gay men in the services, and the fact that in some situations the boundaries became somewhat blurred. I ask Arthur whether he knew of any other gay men among the Guinea Pigs.

'Not at the time,' he tells me, but adds that he has since met another man who was there for a short period after the Battle of Britain. 'But as there were almost seven hundred of us I'm sure there must've been more. You didn't shout it from the rooftops, but there's plenty of evidence that there were gay men in the RAF during the war. Not surprising as a lot of them came straight from the public schools where there was a bit of experimentation going on. If you were seen to do the job, and do it well, it was just assumed you were a normal chap. I did a lot of that ... pretending to be a normal chap—and it was easier on duty than here where everyone was struggling with what had happened to them. Nobody showed it but we were all scared to death about the future and we had too much time on our hands. I think there were a lot of young men reaching out to each other in what I'd call an intimacy of suffering, if I can put it that way. Bonding. So all that flirting and getting off with the nurses was something to do with proving that, despite this very close brotherhood, they were normal chaps. But if you're in a group like that and you're gay, its easy to misread things and that can be risky. Instinctively I knew that, and although I got on well with everyone on the surface I was always watching my step.'

I ask him how he actually managed to merge into that hetero-erotic environment without being challenged. I imagined the laddish culture around the women would have demanded, or at least expected, some sort of involvement and that any man watching silently on the sidelines would have been suspect.

'Oh indeed! I did flirt with the women for just that reason. But I've always thought that somehow nurses sensed I was different even if they hadn't worked out why. Some of the nurses loved all that business, I suppose it was exciting, but there were some who were intimidated and you could see how uncomfortable they were. I remember one sweet little VAD who used to scuttle around with her head down, not making eye contact, as though she was always waiting for the moment she could escape. My sister asked me about this once, a long time ago, and she said that they'd probably have known. So they knew I was a fraud!'

Later I wheel Arthur around the hospital for a while—taking him in to see the honour board, which he studies for several minutes before asking me to take him out into the air again. I park his chair alongside a seat and we talk again as we watch for the return of Angela and Dennis.

'I was in the wrong war,' Arthur says. And I have to ask him to explain.

'All that poetry from the Great War—yearning after the love of lads! But not in our war, all very shameful and dirty then. But y'know history's full of military heroes—Alexander, Frederick the Great, Kitchener, General Gordon, T. E. Lawrence—dozens of 'em, all queer. But as things were in the forces—if you were well connected, and especially if you were a hero, people closed ranks and you were protected.'

I thank him for the time and effort involved in coming here to meet me. 'I wanted to do it,' he says. 'When Angela told me she'd met you, and you'd said you wouldn't use my name I thought I might strike a blow for the gay boys, say that we were there, even if no one realised it. But maybe some of the other men did know. If I'd been a bit older, more experienced, I might have coped better. I used to think about the Jews in Germany, the yellow stars, the armbands, that marked them out. I thought one day someone in the ward would spot me and I'd be finished too.'

Across the car park we see Angela and Dennis getting out of the car. Arthur has told me that Dennis, at seventy-two, is thirteen years younger than him, and they have been together for twenty-seven years. 'He's the love of my life, and has the patience of a saint!' Arthur says. 'Come and see us in Rottingdean.' And by the time they drive off, Dennis has offered to cook Sunday lunch for Angela and me in a couple of weeks' time.

*

Arthur's experience at East Grinstead may or may not be typical of the experience of other gay men who ended up there during the war. He chose to lie low and attempted to demonstrate a sufficient level of heterosexual masculine behaviour to fit in with the dominant culture and expectations. It is impossible to know whether any gay men were less cautious and actually formed liaisons there. I have not found any evidence of this, and that doesn't surprise me. Even Arthur who, more than half a century later, wanted to 'strike a blow for the gay boys', and who has lived as an openly gay man since the 70s, feels unable to 'out' himself in this context.

It has been widely suggested by historians that masculinity during the Great War was tenuous. Trench warfare seemed at odds with the principles of honest combat, it was degrading and squalid, and undermined pre-war expectations of masculinity. By the outbreak of World War II, however, masculinity was being represented in a more traditional terms of aggressive militarism: fit, dynamic young men were matched to machines and weapons that were high tech and high powered. The rhetoric was about men's virility and their quest to fight for and protect women, the home and their country. This frequently created hostility towards, and suspicion of, young men who were required to stay home because they were in reserved occupations. The movement of women into jobs vacated by men who had gone to war increased the tension. Masculinity was crucial to the nation; living up to its standards of action, courage and fearlessness was vital to men themselves and the services as a whole. The very real need for the retention of men in reserved occupations did not protect those who were young from hostility or accusations of cowardice. Men who were not in uniform were either underage, or too old, or—and this was even more difficult—considered unfit. This tended to polarise men to the fit and unfit, and those declared unfit sometimes found themselves facing the slur of cowardice.

Homosexuality was a crime and it attracted heavy penalties including imprisonment and compulsory medical treatments designed to make a man 'normal'. Arthur's tactic of performing to the expectations of masculinity is one that many homosexuals would have adopted. It is interesting, however, that in some areas of the military the old taboos began to crumble during the war and for some the privations and hardship of war, where men lived in close proximity, helped many heterosexual men to recognise that their homosexual colleagues were neither criminals, nor deviants, neither were they cowards. Paul Fussell writes that in the extreme deprivation of the Japanese prison camps homosexual relations were common and not simply as a substitute for sex with women usually described as 'deprivation homosexuality', but relationships grounded in love and trust, and forged in frightful circumstances.[64] Even so, the military was dangerous territory for men who loved men. The temptations were great but getting it wrong could be disastrous. In England attitudes to sexual behaviour remained prudish and puritanical due mainly to the churches, and this cultural puritanism effectively restrained any moves to educate people about their sexuality. It created a miasma of shame, fear and guilt around heterosexuality and sexual activity, along with a disgust, hostility and hatred of homosexuality and, of course, it ensured that the latter remained criminalised.

In the face of overwhelming homophobia it's easy to understand that horribly disfigured young men, desperate to reclaim their masculinity, would seek its confirmation in the company of attractive women, who were encouraged to boost their sense of themselves as men, and frequently as heroes. And it is equally understandable that men who loved men would fear the unpredictable reaction of the dominant group, if their reality became known.

17. FACE OFF

Gordon Brown is not doing well. After a promising start that surprised many of his detractors, his luck has changed, and some of it is to do with his face. Gordon's craggy, homely visage came as a relief after years of a perma-tanned PM, whose pale eyes had begun to look increasingly shifty as he stared into the cameras. Brown's rumpled look was reminiscent of politicians of an earlier era from both major parties. Creased, ill-fitting suits, ties never quite straight, hair sticking out in the wrong places. All he needed was a pipe to fill, and a couple of labradors to walk with on weekends at Chequers, and he could morph into an image of reliable, old-style leadership.

The early polls rose favourably as the new prime minister ploughed doggedly through the challenges of terrorist attacks in London and at Glasgow Airport, the summer floods, and then an outbreak of foot-and-mouth disease. He looked serious and solid, a no-bullshit prime minister, that safe pair of hands. Even Gordon sceptics who could not forgive him for decisions made as chancellor, were warming to him. But now the honeymoon is over. There have been gaffes, and poor decisions, a failure to communicate a distinctive message. Deprived of charisma, the fickle electorate wants it back: just a sliver of warmth, a humorous quip, some glimpse of a humble, cuddly Gordon – and please – an occasional smile?

It's shocking how decades of media exposure have made us expect political leaders to perform as celebrities in front of the cameras. How quick we are to criticise a facial or verbal idiosyncrasy, to read shiftiness into a sideways glance. In just a few months Gordon's popularity is on the downward slope. Part of the problem is that he is not delivering in the celebrity performance stakes. His shortcomings are becoming increasingly obvious: his inability to smile, to laugh on cue, to twinkle and flirt, Blair-like, with the cameras, to chuckle lightheartedly, to vary and soften his expression. The trouble is that his face simply doesn't work.

Gordon Brown's face problem began in his late teens when he was felled by a kick in the head during a school rugby match. It left him with a detached retina in his left eye. For weeks he lay flat on his back in a darkened room undergoing treatment, including four operations, all to no avail. The injury robbed him of the sight in that eye. A few years later, while a student at the University of Edinburgh, he began to experience similar problems in his right eye while playing tennis, and was soon back in surgery. His sight was saved, but one of the operations had robbed him of something else—the ability to produce a spontaneous smile. The muscles of his face no longer responded to his attempts to smile; smiling hurts, worse still it produces a grin that cracks and distorts his face. It is a grin that lacks warmth, a gash of a grin like a splash of acid, when what is needed is a smile of reassurance. In a man whose pleasantly craggy face shows no obvious signs of injury—no scars, no repairs, no obvious disfigurements—the struggle to smile, which includes the appearance of chewing something unpleasant before the gash-grin appears, has always been a problem. And it's a problem that can pass for a while but, with increased media exposure, it has become a major impediment to communicating trust in difficult times.

In *Alice through the Looking Glass* Alice remarks to Humpty Dumpty that 'the face is what one goes by, generally'.

'That's just what I complain of,' Humpty Dumpty replies. 'Your face is the same as everybody has—the two eyes, so—' (marking their places in the air with his thumb) 'nose in the middle, mouth under. It's always the same. Now if you had the two eyes on the same side of the nose, for instance—or the mouth at the top—that would be SOME help.'

'It wouldn't look nice,' is Alice's retort to Humpty Dumpty, who simply closes his eyes and replies, 'Wait until you've tried it.'[65]

Alice is right: we have expectations about appearance, especially in relation to faces, and our tolerance of the unexpected, the non-conforming, can be limited. Gordon's struggle with his face is his misfortune, for his struggle is read as ill temper, lack of humour, dismissiveness where there should be tolerance, scorn where there should be empathy. Gordon's grin is eerily similar to the grin of the Guinea Pig as he stepped off the bus all those years ago.

Humpty Dumpty's 'wait until you've tried it' is a challenge to experiment with the monstrous, to reverse, shuffle, shift and swing the expected into a form of 'otherness'. But some people have otherness thrust upon them and are forced to live with it. A study of the faces of flyers who were burned, mashed or fried is a study of monstrosity, something so outrageous that it is unbearable. Plastic surgery rescued them from monstrosity and abjection, but the many operations, the pedicles, the cutting and layering, have demanded a lifetime of patience, of reliving the injuries and traumas of reconstruction over and over again; a lifetime's work to escape monstrosity, to minimise difference and to reclaim the relief of ordinariness. In another war they would have rotted by the roadside, begging for a living, as ordinary faces turned away from them in fear and ignorance. McIndoe's boys had to face ignorance and prejudice during and after their war. Their injuries were often assumed to be hereditary and they were asked if their appearance might be passed on to their children. And the age-old association of facial disfigurement with madness and evil awaited them round every corner.

Gordon Brown's facial muscles won't follow instructions and the result frequently makes him look wrong, inappropriate. Bill Foxley's face muscles have been destroyed. He can't smile, his eyes don't work and yet somehow he is *always* appropriate. His eyes can't look out and others can't look in but somehow the essence of the man and what he wants to express is always present. Humpty Dumpty would easily recognise Dennis Neale, but with his eyes at different levels Dennis looks out on the world in a way that transcends difference. Today the techniques that saved the lives and the sanity of McIndoe's patients are used to correct facial 'faults' that most of us don't even see.

Cosmetic surgery today abhors difference. It erases the lines and folds of character and age, it stretches and perfects, so that the faces of young women, in particular, look more and more alike: similar noses, straight white teeth, plumped lips, and the bland appearance of having just been rolled off the assembly line. In doing so it creates a different kind of unnatural plasticised monstrosity.

Back again in Evelyn's kitchen we are talking about faces, about the assumptions we make about character and personality based on a person's face: the disadvantage of not being able to move the face or of having one that misrepresents its owner's intentions. We discuss the awkwardness of bumping into a friend whom we haven't seen for a while and finding ourselves face to face with a new nose, eyelids that have been lifted, or smooth, stretched skin where once were wrinkles. How should we react? Should we comment, ask a question, pretend we haven't noticed?

'Sometimes,' Evelyn says, 'I feel slightly offended, I try to look away and I'm always uncomfortable. I want her to be what she was before, wrinkles, droopy eyelids, a nose that looked okay to me.'

I know what she means. There is a slight sense of betrayal and then unease, the facial work stands between us until we can learn to adjust to the new face. So what is it like if the face is not simply adjusted, but destroyed, changed so dramatically as to be unrecognisable? What if that face is the one you have kissed goodnight, and woken up to each morning and loved? And how does it feel to be transformed by facial disfigurement and see strangers, and more importantly, loved ones, respond to you with dismay and disgust?

*

In his memoir *Shot Down in Flames*, Wing Commander (then Pilot Officer) Geoffrey Page describes his first glimpse of his damaged face, which came as he lay on the operating table in the RAF hospital in Halton. It was 1940 and Page was flying a Hawker Hurricane when he was hit by enemy fire that exploded the fuel tank and he was enveloped in flames. He struggled to release himself from the safety harness and escaped from the cockpit, parachute intact, and began his descent into the sea in sight of the Kent coast, near Margate, with the sickening smell of his own burned flesh in his nostrils. Page was in agony when a British merchant ship eventually picked him up. At Halton, as he waited in the operating theatre for the anaesthetic needle, he glanced up and caught sight of himself in the reflector mirrors. 'My last conscious memory was of seeing the hideous mass of swollen burnt flesh that had once been a face.'

Page goes on to describe his first major setback that followed the relief of being alive. A VAD – 'one of the prettiest girls I'd seen in all my life' – came to assist with the dressings on his hands. 'She personified the wounded warrior's idea of the ideal angel of mercy,' but the young nurse was unable to disguise 'the expression of horror and loathing' when she saw his injuries. 'I longed for beauty to cast me a friendly glance, even if it came in the shabby guise of pity, but the first expression remained constant.' When he asked the senior nurse for a mirror the request was steadfastly refused and when she had left, Page steeled himself to get out of bed and look in the mirror. It took him more than five minutes to manage the two steps from the bed to the basin and, once there, to close his eyes tightly to clear the moisture that constantly gathered in them. 'The shock of the swollen face three times its normal size was almost too great to comprehend, but it was weakness and not horror that caused me to faint away.'[66]

Had Page been at East Grinstead at the time, the young VAD would immediately have been sent elsewhere. While some experienced nurses were prepared for the faces that looked up at them from beds and stretchers, others had no idea what to expect.

Jane Lyons, who went to East Grinstead as a VAD in 1940, recalls her shock when on her first day she looked down at the face of a man who had just been admitted. 'It was mashed to a pulp. There was a hole where his right eye should have been, the other eye was sort of lying on his cheek. The bottom half of his face had been jammed sideways and his teeth were smashed and sticking out at all different angles. I'd just been lectured about not letting my face show anything, but I'm sure it must have shown, so perhaps no one noticed. I just turned around and went to the toilets and wept. It was a tough start.'

Despite this, Jane loved her two years at the hospital. 'I'd say that it only took a couple of weeks to be able to look at the worst injuries, and then it became the most wonderful time of my life. After a while you just saw through the wounds and burns to the person. We were frightfully naughty of course, those boys were desperate to feel loved and accepted, and we were too. This might shock you, my dear, but a lot of sex went on there. I was a virgin, but that didn't last long! At first I was a bit nervous about it all, but I proved to be a fast learner.' Jane, now eighty-three, lets out a big guffaw of laughter as she tells me this. 'And apparently I got very good at it. You asked me just now if I felt I was coerced into sex, well yes I was, the first few times. But it seemed like just going that bit further in caring for them. I started off feeling it was my war effort, but soon I was doing it not just for the war or the men, but for myself. I discovered sex there, and I got to love those boys, they were heroes and it made me feel good that I could make them feel better about themselves.'

Although Jane lacked sexual experience before she went to East Grinstead she says she was very confident as a girl and had been encouraged towards independence and to speak up for herself at home. Unlike some of the other young, untrained nurses, she came from a wealthy family whom she describes as 'upper-class'. 'I'd have been presented at court, if the war hadn't ruined it. I had a privileged background, I always felt confident that I would be able to manage anything. I was never timid.'

For some women though, the facial injuries of men whom they loved were simply too much to bear. Emily Mayhew had told me how wives and girlfriends, arriving to visit their injured men for the first time, sometimes turned away in horror, leaving the hospital and never coming back.

Some women refused to recognise and claim unidentified unconscious men who had arrived in the hospital and whose identities could not be established. Burned hands have no fingerprints, smashed and toothless jaws distort the shape of the face, noses that are burned away and empty eye sockets, meant that a terrified girlfriend could easily slip away by failing to identify the patient. Some women made an effort to hide their distaste and distress for a few visits but then those visits faded out, engagements were broken off, marriages were quietly dissolved and hearts were broken on both sides of the divide.

Squadron Leader William Simpson was shot down in France in 1940, and spent almost a year in hospital there before he was repatriated to England. His hands and face were severely burned and throughout his time there he dreamed of coming home and once again seeing his wife, Hope, whom he had married in 1939. In his memoir *I Burned My Fingers*, Simpson provides a graphic description of the agony of the inadequate treatment, the cramped, dirty conditions, the swarms of flies drawn to the wounds, and the torture of having dressings changed made more agonising by being left too long. At one point when dressings on his hands were changed, they were found to be alive with maggots. By the time he was evacuated from France and sent back to England he was aware that his face, although healed, was 'heavily and lumpily scarred and was stretched and drawn about the mouth giving me a twisted smile and a receding chin'. His nose was blotchy, red and white, and swollen. The lids of his left eye were missing and it watered constantly, and his nose was 'reduced and tapered to a point and one nostril wing was missing.'[67] He could walk but was unable to bend his left knee, and the stump that remained of his left hand was fully bandaged, and part bandaging on the right hand revealed two charred stumps of fingers. He had, by this time, trained himself not to care about what he knew was his 'odd and forbidding appearance'. The acceptance and affection he had enjoyed with some French nurses had convinced him that women 'cared nothing for scars and crippling wounds provided that the essential manhood in a man's spirit—and presumably also in his body—was unimpaired.' So, although he realised that Hope would be shocked by his injuries, particularly the horrible transformation of his hands, he believed that she would come to terms with them. As he made his way to meet her at a hotel in Weston-Super-Mare, Simpson was unaware that Hope had not been advised of the extent or nature of his injuries.

'All the horror she had always suffered at the sight of blood and mutilation spread through her like a fever, and she broke down and wept. It was bitterly ironical that this instinctive compassion hardened me against her, and the spiritual and physical links that had bound us together snapped.' His heart, he says, 'turned to stone.'[68] The couple spent the weekend together with some difficulty, and did manage to establish some sense of warmth, but the relationship did not recover. They were later divorced and after treatment at East Grinstead, Simpson returned to service in the RAF. After the war he married again, started a family and eventually became the Press and Information Officer for the (then) British European Airways.

But there were compensations for some Guinea Pigs. Foremost among these was the presence of the nurses, and of other women whom they met in McIndoe-controlled situations both at the hospital, on social occasions and when convalescing locally and at Marchwood Park.

Mary Perry met her future husband, Jack, at a dance at Marchwood Park. 'Before we'd finished the first dance I knew he was special,' she told me. Jack had been called up in 1943 at the age of seventeen and wanted to become a pilot, but was redirected to training as a flight engineer due to his pre-war apprenticeship. He passed out in 1944 and after only two raids was wounded in a crash caused by a nut on the outlet side of the fuel pump being only finger-tight, not locked by a spanner and wired. The tail gunner was killed, Jack's face and hands were badly burned, and there were patches of burns on his legs. He was sent first to a special RAF Burns Unit at Rauceby Hospital in Sheffield and, in 1946, to East Grinstead.

It was during one of his periods of convalescence that he and Mary met.

'I was never too much worried by their injuries,' Mary says. 'I used to go up there to dances and we all had a lovely time, and then one time I met Jack. I felt I could see who he was despite his face, in fact I thought he was lovely, that's what I could see beyond the damage, and I was right.'

Some women, she told me, could always see through it, but many could not. 'And I don't think that was something they could change,' she says. 'You're either able to do it or you're not, and I was lucky because I could see Jack, who he really was, and we fell in love and we've been together ever since.'

Ella Morgan has a similar view, although her then fiancé Alan's face was not damaged but his hands were in a terrible state. It was Alan who had arrived in Ward III thinking he was in a nuthouse. He began his working life as an apprentice toolmaker and his attempt to join the navy at the outbreak of war had been knocked back. As a skilled worker he was in a reserved occupation and considered more valuable on the shop floor with Cooper Ferguson, manufacturing parts for the new Lancaster bombers. He had to wait until 1942 when Churchill proposed a new strategic bombing offensive designed to attack German cities, and Air Marshal Sir Arthur 'Bomber' Harris was appointed Commander-in-Chief of Bomber Command. By then the loss of so many men led to those in reserved occupations being called up. Alan was sent for training as a flight engineer, and then to the Operational Training Unit at Swinderby, leaving his girlfriend, Ella, at home in Manchester. The two had met four years earlier in the works canteen when Alan was seventeen and Ella fifteen, and had been together ever since. Three months later, when Alan was the flight engineer on a Lancaster on a bombing mission to Stuttgart and Leipzig, the aircraft was attacked by enemy fire and a side door burst open. Two aircrew who attempted to close the door rapidly passed out from lack of oxygen and Alan managed to pull them to safety and connect them to the oxygen supply. He then lost consciousness himself and collapsed with his hands hanging outside the still open door.

It was his fourteenth mission in three months, and the eve of his twenty-first birthday.

In Ward III, surrounded by men wounded and traumatised by fire, Alan Morgan was suffering from frostbite. McIndoe attempted to rescue his hands, which had been incorrectly treated elsewhere, but the damage was too severe. He had no option but to amputate the fingers.

'Until then I had some hope,' Alan says 'but that finished me. I was a skilled tradesman with two fingerless hands, what good was I? And I was bloody sure Ella wouldn't want to marry me. I had no future, nothing to live for.' Alan sank into depression, his physical condition deteriorated rapidly and the staff feared for his life. It was two weeks later that Ella got news of him from the hospital.

'He hadn't come home for his twenty-first birthday and I was worried,' she told me over tea at their home in Romiley, near Manchester. 'He didn't let me know because he thought I wouldn't want him anymore. I was at work when I got the message. They said he was very poorly and it was fifty-fifty whether he'd get through it and it might help if I could get down there as soon as possible.' Ella caught a midnight train from Manchester, changed at Crewe for Euston, took the underground to Victoria and the train to East Grinstead, and walked all the way from the station to the hospital. I was that terrified he'd have died before I got there. I'll never forget that journey.'

Alan was shocked when Ella arrived at his bedside. 'I think I said—what are you here for? You won't want me now. But she just told me not to be so daft. "We're getting married," she says, "and you'd better hurry up and get better because I'm planning the wedding".'

Within a week of Ella's arrival, it was clear that Alan was going to live; his condition had improved dramatically. 'She gave me hope, you see. I told her I'd never be able to make a living, never work. "Well I can work," she said, "we'll manage."'

After the operation to amputate his fingers it was of little comfort to Alan to learn that McIndoe had managed to save a part of each thumb, which would help in restoring the use of his hands. It was only later that he realised how vital those stumps of thumbs would become, and how significant his time in the 'nuthouse' of Ward III would be in restoring that future.

Ella Morgan understood instinctively what McIndoe had established in Ward III and how crucial it was to his patients' recovery. She understood Alan's need to be as good as his colleagues in the workplace, to serve his country in the war, and to provide for her and the family they hoped to have. And she never underestimated her own role and responsibility for helping him to regain that sense of purpose and overcome the challenges ahead.

'I talked to people there, the nurses, you know, and they said some of the men—their wives or girlfriends—well—they just couldn't face it. They'd just go away, not even go into the ward. Well you think of that, and the men they'd just lose all hope. So, I told him we were getting married. I had to show him that we were going to have a life together, give him something to look forward to.'

Alan and Ella were married four months later and Ella believed she could be the breadwinner, or that they might perhaps run a shop together. She took lodgings locally and moved to East Grinstead to be nearer Alan; there she helped out on Ward III, regularly feeding Bill Foxley and others until Alan was discharged. 'I kept telling him, you're lucky, look at the others with their terrible burned faces. We'll be all right. I could see it happen all the time, some women could cope, they could look at those terribly burned faces and see who was in there, but others, they just couldn't. And I wouldn't want to blame anyone for that. We're all individuals. I think I'd've been all right if Alan's face were burned. He were always himself to me, hands or not. But you can only do what you're capable of, can't you? But it were very sad for the men.'

During the early part of the war, after the Battle of Britain, the government, horrified by the extent of the facial disfigurement of so many air crew, decided that they would have to be hidden at a secret location to avoid frightening ordinary people. McIndoe would have none of it. Each year during his lifetime the club invited its hero, Sir Winston Churchill, to attend the reunion, but Churchill never came. Years later it was revealed that on the orders of Lady Churchill the invitations were never shown to him. She wanted to protect him from coming face to face with these men who wore the all too obvious cost of some of his wartime policies.

18. EMOTIONAL LABOUR AND WAR WORK

Alice lives in a small village outside Watford; she is Joyce's friend, and when I first called her a few weeks ago she was due to go into hospital. Now she is home and willing to talk to me.

'But I might change my mind halfway through, would I be able to do that?' she asks on the phone.

I explain that this is fine, that even general background is useful, and if she doesn't want me to write about her personal experiences then she only has to say so.

'And my name?'

'You can use another name.'

'Well if you're sure ...'

'I'm sure,' I tell her. 'And if, when I arrive, you've changed your mind then that's fine too.'

On the way to meet Alice I visit nearby Bricket Wood where I lived for four years in the early 70s after my first marriage broke down. I pull up outside the bungalow where, as a single woman with two boys aged two and six, I started a different life. The bungalow is smarter now, and another room has been added. I have thought of this place and our time here as a turning point, a period when, at thirty, I had to get to grips with life without a safety net. My parents, who had retired to Spain a few years earlier, had been horrified that I'd left my husband, and severed contact with me for several years. It was the first time in my life that I felt entirely alone and unsupported. Maintenance payments were minimal and I needed a job that was manageable for a sole parent. But my overwhelming memories of that time are not of the financial struggle, nor the times I woke in the night sweating with fear about where I would find the money to pay the electricity bill, or the weekly cost of childcare. What I remember are my neighbours, Anne and Tony and their three boys, similar in age to my own. I remember how they were always there for me, to laugh with and cry on. How Tony took down a section of the dividing fence so the boys could run freely between the two gardens. I remember the kids playing together in sunshine and in deep snow, and the time that Anne and I took them on holiday to a cottage in Lyme Regis, and made up stupid rhymes for them in the car. They were people to whom it seemed quite natural to go that little bit further, to always do a bit more as though it was no trouble at all. We graduated from neighbourliness to a friendship rooted in their rare generosity of spirit.

Later I meet them for lunch in St Albans and we spend a couple of hours swapping memories, and laughing until we cry over the joys and dramas of raising sons. Just before we leave the restaurant, their son Richard arrives with his wife. He is the oldest of the boys, and was always a steady, responsible presence. Now in his early forties, that steadiness and reliability is still obvious and I notice that he is watching us with quiet amusement. His expression is indulgent and slightly puzzled, in a way in which I know I have regarded much older people, while thinking how weird but endearing they are. Recognising this is, for me, a marker of the shift in relationships. In this place and time Richard seems to represent not only his brothers but also my two sons—no longer boys, not even particularly young men, a generation who rightly see us as something separate—the oldies. We are a place where they know they are eventually heading, but prefer to keep that at a safe distance. It is a pleasant and rather touching experience.

Alice lives in a small retirement complex, and the neat square of her front garden is home to a large collection of colourful garden gnomes.

'For some reason my grandson thinks I like them, and keeps buying them for me. I haven't the heart to tell him ...' she explains.

Alice, slight and small-boned, with pure white hair and dazzling blue eyes, looks much younger than her eighty-four years. In 1939 she was living in Brighton with her parents and celebrated her seventeenth birthday a few weeks before war was declared.

'I wanted to join the navy,' she told me, 'but my father wouldn't have a bar of it. He said it wasn't a proper thing for a nice girl to do. He was a lovely man, a bit domineering, but very kind and always concerned about respectability. He was a senior clerk with the bank and quite a lot older than Mum, so he wasn't called up. They were both very religious and quite strict about what I could and couldn't do. But they did let me go and help with the blackout, you know painting out the windows in some of the buildings, with some other girls, but Dad wouldn't entertain me going into the services.'

Eventually it became clear that young women would need to volunteer for war work or be called up and Alice's parents agreed that volunteering as a VAD would be better than being drafted into the services or a factory.

'The Red Cross organised all the training, it was about three months as I remember. And it was pretty basic. Mostly we learned on the job.' Late in 1940 Alice was sent to a hospital in Surrey, located in a large house.

'It was winter and the thing I remember most was how cold it was because it was a big old house with no heating, and we slept in huts with no doors and no electricity. I used to get into my sleeping bag wrapped in all my outdoor clothes, and once I got warm I tried not to move in case I let cold air in. I wonder the patients didn't die of cold, especially when we gave them blanket baths, because by the time we got the hot water to them up lots of stairs and passages, it was almost cold. I quite liked it there apart from the cold. I got on well with the other nurses and the sisters.'

The following summer Alice's parents moved from Brighton to live with her grandparents just outside East Grinstead. 'My grandmother was ill and my granddad was even worse and they couldn't manage alone anymore. There was a job going in the East Grinstead branch of the bank and Dad was able to move there.'

It was just a few months later that Alice too was transferred to East Grinstead.

'I was a bit torn about it because although I'd missed my parents I was enjoying having a life of my own,' she says. 'And I liked being with the other girls. East Grinstead was very different. The sisters and the other nurses were lovely, and so was Matron, but I was scared of Mr McIndoe. I wanted to run and hide whenever I saw him – not that he was ever unkind to me or anything, it's just how he was.'

'And the patients,' I ask. 'How did you get on with them?'

'Most of them were very nice, and you'd look at their poor faces and think you wanted to do anything to make them feel better. But it was difficult.' Alice pauses and I think that perhaps she is going to stop at this point, but she continues. 'It was how it was set up – was the problem. Mr McIndoe wanted them to have everything their own way as long as he thought it was all right. Nobody, not even Matron, could do anything about it, and they had been through something terrible, you could understand that. They were stuck there, having operation after operation. I could see it mattered that we girls sort of played up to them, it made them feel better. They showed off a lot, moving beds around, hiding things from us, bedpans, charts that sort of thing. I'd grown up with a lot of rules about how to behave, and I enjoyed being away from some of the petty rules at home. The first hospital had its own rules and they were sometimes a bit much but rules in a way make you feel safe. You know where you are, so to speak. If there were rules for the patients at East Grinstead, you never knew what they were because they seemed to do whatever suited them and they egged each other on. You know what men are like, especially when there are young women around. If you didn't join in with them they'd tease you.'

I ask Alice how she was able to handle it, and the pause is so long that I think she's not going to answer.

'I used to dread going to work. I felt so sorry for them because of what they'd been through, but I was upset by things they did. I felt I was being pressured to ... well to behave in a way that went against everything my parents had taught me. Some girls coped all right, they enjoyed it, but I'd never been with a man. I mean, not even been out with one. I only half understood what was going on. I was afraid of getting pushed into something I didn't want.'

I ask Alice if she told her parents how she felt. She laughs and shakes her head. 'Oh dear no,' she says. 'I couldn't do that. You see Mr McIndoe and the patients, they were so special. My dad knew all about them from the bank, and Mum knew about them from my grandparents. People in the town were all out for the patients, and Mr McIndoe was a really important person. You couldn't say anything negative about what went on. I didn't dare tell my parents, because I was sure that they'd think it was my fault—like I'd been flirting, or encouraging them somehow. So I just sort of carried on, kept my head down and tried to pretend I didn't mind.'

Once, when she was on a night duty, a patient coming back from the pub somewhat the worse for drink, dragged her into an unlit passage and tried to bully her into having sex with him. It was, she says, a rough encounter, and she ended up with bruises on her arms.

'He was a man I'd never liked, quite a lot older than most of them. I managed to get away from him, because he knocked against a shelf and stuff fell off and he tripped. I couldn't stop shaking. The night sister asked what was the matter and I just said I didn't feel well. She was very kind and made me tea and took my temperature, but I didn't dare tell her what had happened.'

When Alice got home at the end of her shift her mother was out and so she went straight to bed. And when it was time to go back on the night shift she feigned sickness. 'I didn't want to go to work in case he'd said something about it, you know, with the others, because they'd tease me about it. I didn't dare tell Mum so I pretended I was ill and hid in bed for a week.' But eventually she had to go back to work. 'He ignored me after that, thank goodness, and I don't think he'd said anything. But I was always nervous around him. Now I wonder if he was so drunk he didn't remember he'd done it, or perhaps didn't remember which nurse it was. We all had to do our bit for the war so I had to get on and do mine. Now I'm older I think they didn't mean any harm, except that one of course, and none of the girls liked him. But we put up with a lot. One of the older nurses said "just think of it as your war work", and I tried to do that but it didn't really help.'

I drive back from Watford thinking over what Alice has told me, particularly her concern that her parents might blame her for the men's behaviour or suggest she had encouraged it. Joyce had said something similar, as had two women to whom I had spoken on the phone. They had both enjoyed their time at East Grinstead and found it a liberating experience both sexually and in terms of their careers. Even so both had said they feared being 'found out' and blamed by their families or others, for the patients' behaviour. This makes sense in the wider context of concern that was being expressed about women's behaviour in wartime. Sonya Rose writes that 'During World War II there was widespread public apprehension about the declining morals of girls and young women in British cities and towns.' This anxiety was sufficient to cause considerable debate in the newspapers and in Parliament in the early years of the war.[69] So it is easy to see why women feared that speaking out about behaviour that made them uncomfortable could be turned back on them.

Holding women responsible for men's behaviour was not new then, and is still alive and well today. And this aspect of the women's stories chimes with an experience of my own which took place years later. In July 1960 I left school at the age of sixteen and spent the next year taking a secretarial course at nearby technical college. In 1961, with poor typing and worse shorthand, I got my first job with a small import-export company with cramped offices high up in a building in London's Park Lane.

I set off on the train that first week bursting with excitement about the possibilities of being a working girl in London. I imagined making new, more sophisticated friends, maybe eventually sharing a flat with other girls, and escaping my parents' vigilance. It was a difficult first week due to my shyness and lack of experience, but everyone was very friendly, and told me about a party due that Friday evening, with clients arriving from somewhere in Europe. When it was discovered that I spoke quite good French, I was told I'd be very useful and popular on Friday night.

As I left the office on the Thursday evening one of the older girls joined me in the lift. She was an attractive outgoing young woman in her late twenties, with a fashionable 'beehive' hairdo. I thought she was the epitome of glamour, as though she had stepped out of the pages of a fashion magazine. As we strolled out of the building she nudged me in the ribs.

'See you tomorrow, don't forget to bring your overnight bag!'

'Oh, I'll be getting the ten o'clock train home,' I said and was amazed when she burst out laughing.

'No blossom. We're staying the night, all of us. Why do you think they want us girls there? Not for our shorthand that's for sure. And you with your lovely French speaking ...'

And she went on to explain that the girls spent the night with clients and often got gifts, or a little 'cash in hand'.

On the train home, my head was spinning with panic, my face burning with embarrassment. I felt as though the people in the carriage could read my thoughts and I couldn't understand how I had ended up in this situation. Was there some sort of suggestion of this during the job interview? I went back over everything that had happened at work that week but could think of nothing that I had missed that might have warned me about this expectation. One thing I knew for sure was that I was never going to tell my parents, because they would think it was my fault; that others must have assumed from my behaviour that I would be a part of this. I imagined my father asking sternly what I had done to encourage this. I believe now that this was most unlikely, but at the time it was paralysing. I barely slept that night and left for work as usual the following morning. But instead of going on to London I got off the train at Croydon and spent the day wandering around the shops, sitting in a park, and drinking cups of tea in cafés until it was time to go home again. It was over one of those cups of tea that I decided on an escape route. I arrived home at the usual time and told my parents I had got the sack because my shorthand was so bad. My father was disappointed, I must work harder to improve my skills, he said. My mother on the other hand was relieved.

'You're far too young to be on your own in London,' she said, glaring at Dad. 'I told your father he shouldn't encourage you. Goodness knows who might take advantage of you. You must get a job nearer to home.'

I never did tell them the truth about this, and for years I was scared of finding myself in a situation where something that a man might do without my consent would end up being my fault.

*

Ten days after my meeting with Alice, I have afternoon tea in a flat in Paddington with Celia Hewett who spent eight months on Ward III in 1944. She was twenty-five at the time and now lives with her daughter Judy. It is Judy who called me, having heard from someone in East Grinstead that I was looking for nurses. Celia has a problem with mobility and is largely confined to a wheelchair, but she has no trouble recalling her time at East Grinstead.

'Wonderful,' she tells me, 'I was working in Sir Harold Gillies' hospital—plastic surgery too of course, and I wanted a bit of a change. I'd heard about Mr McIndoe and East Grinstead, and I had a boyfriend who had a car and petrol to put in it. So I got him to drive me to East Grinstead on my day off. I just walked in to Mr McIndoe's office and told him I wanted a job. He looked a bit surprised, but I got the job.'

I ask her about the behaviour of the patients and the way the ward was run.

'It was difficult sometimes,' she says, 'the injuries were unbelievable of course but I was pretty well immune to that by then. And obviously I was confident or I would never have turned up at the hospital like that. I had enough experience to be able to handle the patients, unlike some of the girls. It was so different from what I expected and I loved those men. And yes, I know what you're talking about and some of what went on was a bit X-rated but there was no harm in it. It was a wonderful experience. I'm still in touch with one of them. Ten years ago Judy took me to Canada and we stayed with him and his wife in Montreal. They were wonderful times. Sir Archibald was my hero. He was a tyrant and a saint all in together.'

Clearly the ways in which the women I met experienced Ward III are polarised. All of them found the work and the environment challenging. Their responses to the culture, the atmosphere of flirtation, the general lack of rules for the patients and their expectations, are individual and personal. I was only able to trace a few of the many women who nursed the Guinea Pigs and, irrespective of their personal experience, all spoke with admiration and respect for the men themselves, their courage and spirit. Even those who have bad memories of the time retain affection for their patients. And all of them were concerned that whatever they said, and what I wrote as a result, should not tarnish the Guinea Pigs' reputations, or that of the surgeon. Most wanted anonymity so that no one would know who had been 'telling tales'—a term which several used at some stage. And some saw their own difficulty in accommodating the men's 'pranks' as a failing on their own part. Going beyond the usual boundaries of nursing was often discussed as their 'war work' or 'doing my bit for the war'.

In the 1980s, Arlie Russell Hochschild, Professor of Sociology at the University of California, Berkley, began a study on how human beings manage emotions, particularly in the workplace. Her initial study was carried out with flight attendants and investigated the ways in which they were groomed to perform in ways that reflected the airline's disposition. Smiling, for example, had to be genuine, not just pasted on. The women, and they were nearly all women in those days, were trained to change the way they felt in order to make that smile genuine. They were trained to smile even when dealing with the most obnoxious drunk and abusive passengers. Their role, they were told, was not just to be polite and serve meals, not just to pretend, but to change their own feelings so that they would deliver what the airline's advertisement promised: 'not just smiles and service but travel experience of real happiness and calm.'[70] Hochschild points out that all social interaction involves attempts to signal feelings through devices such as a welcoming or reassuring smile, a laugh that suggests agreement, a nod of assent or affirmation. These are things that we all do every day and which she describes as 'emotional work'. It is a deliberate process that we employ to produce appropriate or acceptable emotions in others. We do it in friendships and relationships with those around us, and we know this behaviour by heart because it is what facilitates our interactions with others and cements our relationships with those close to us. When this emotional work is incorporated into paid labour and is a core element of the job, Hochschild defines it as 'emotional labour'. This sort of 'labour' is central to jobs in the service and caring sectors in which the employee is required to produce a particular emotional state in the client or patient. 'This kind of labor,' Hochschild suggests, 'calls for a co-ordination of mind and feeling, and it sometimes draws on a source of self that we honour as deep and integral to our individuality.'[71] Hochschild maintains that emotional work in personal life is grounded in 'deep acting', which is a natural result of working on our feelings—it becomes spontaneous. In contrast, emotional labour in the workplace is based on 'surface acting' in which we try to change how we outwardly appear. And Hochschild cites ways in which employers attempt to influence the imagination of staff in terms of how they might feel or think about difficult customers and difficult health care clients.[72] Since those early studies Hochschild and others have conducted similar studies on other jobs and professions including nursing.

In most cases they discovered that nurses, like many other caring professionals, are not normally closely supervised in their emotion work with patients or clients. Within the confines of their profession and patient expectations their skilled status allows them to retain autonomy over how they carry out the emotional part of their job. But nurses indicate that they can demonstrate a professional and personal approach to their work and that the two may come into conflict, creating increased levels of 'emotional labour'.[73] One study reports that 'nurses often adopt a feminine script, eschewing professional feeling rules and offering additional gestures of care that they believe are central to any definition of good nursing'.[74] Emotional labour in which people try to change their surface acting in order to change how they appear involves a challenge to the sense of self, and it comes at a cost. 'A principle of *emotive dissonance,* analogous to the principle of cognitive dissonance, is at work. Maintaining a difference between feeling and feigning over the long run leads to strain. We try to reduce this strain by pulling the two closer together either by changing what we feel or changing what we feign. When display is what is required by a job, it is usually feeling that has to change; and when conditions estrange us from our faces they sometimes estrange us from feeling as well.'[75]

Archibald McIndoe's expectations of his nurses meant that changing feeling was, for many, essential. The demanding task of nursing burns patients, under the unusually difficult and complex professional and emotional circumstances in Ward III, created confusion about boundaries, professionalism and suppression of feelings. It was a job that demanded high levels of nursing skill, compassion and a degree of emotional labour, which for some, proved a challenge to their sense of themselves and left them with a disturbing sense of unease and anxiety which they found impossible to share with others.

'I think Sir Archibald would have liked every nurse to fall in love with and marry a Guinea Pig,' a nurse told me. And of course some did.

But it needs to be remembered that while some of the nurses were very young, inexperienced in the work and innocent and ignorant when it came to sex, so too were many of the men who went to war in their late teens and had their youth cut away from them, leaving them to face a future that seemed hopeless. Some, indeed most, of McIndoe's 'boys' really were just boys, the same age as many of the nurses. In different times and situations much of what happened between them would not have been unusual. The difference is that in a workplace where there was pressure to conform to the dominant culture, some young women were not equipped to deal with the situation. For some, it was professionally rewarding and a liberating experience; others felt damaged and shamed by it and there was no mechanism of support to help them through that. Caring for Guinea Pigs was a labour of love on the part of all the nurses; and some of those who struggled with the work environment and the attitude of McIndoe and his boys, explain their confusion and sometimes uneasy compliance as 'doing that bit more for the war'.

19. BACK TO WORK

Alan Morgan counts himself lucky. As Ella pointed out to him during the early days in Ward III, his hands were a mess but he was surrounded by men whose faces had been burned and broken, and many had lost part or all of their sight. But Alan didn't feel lucky. The frostbite had taken eight of his fingers. He was twenty-one and each time he thought of the future he saw himself as useless, unable to work, and a burden on the people who loved him. With one full thumb and one half thumb he had little faith in the shallow clefts that McIndoe and his team had made around the knuckle joints of the fingers to allow for some movement. But Ella urged him on and he spent hours, every day for months, wearing out dozens of pencils as he practised writing his name. Slowly he built up mobility in his joints and eventually managed to persuade McIndoe and the RAF medical board that he could return to the service. He wanted to get back in the air, and to serve long enough to make promotion to flight sergeant, and he did just that, spending his last months in the RAF as a flight engineer. The extraordinary dexterity he had achieved with his stumps also impressed his pre-war employers and when he was demobbed, Alan returned to his original job. Ella, meanwhile, opened a small shop and the couple seemed set for the future, to the point where Ella eventually gave up the shop to concentrate on their family.

It wasn't long after this that Alan's employer was taken over by another company and he was made redundant. Prospective employers took one look at his hands and shook their heads, and although he begged for the chance to demonstrate his dexterity he was consistently denied the opportunity to do so.

It was a dark period for the Morgans; Alan was at the end of his tether and deeply depressed. In this state of mind he didn't realise that the Guinea Pig Club could help him; it had already taken a forceful stand with employers for other members, but Alan had not kept in touch and the future looked grim. Eventually, as the situation grew worse he got himself to an interview.

'I just kept me hands in me pockets,' he says. 'Managed to do that the whole time I was there, and I got the job. Then a few days after I started work the boss comes up me and says, "You never told me about your hands." So I just said, "Well, am I doing the job all right?" And he said I was. And that was the last I heard about it, no one mentioned my hands after that.' Alan was a jig borer once again and proud to be able to work to 0.00015 of an inch on the jig boring machine. It was something he never dreamed he'd achieve when he first discovered the truth about his hands in Ward III.

Every Guinea Pig had to overcome extraordinary physical, psychological and emotional obstacles on the road to new personal and working lives. Hands burned to stumps, lost fingers, amputations, and impairment of mobility looked even more grim for men who were also facially disfigured, and in addition some had also lost wives or girlfriends. Archibald McIndoe was determined that everything possible would be done to prepare them for life after the war and after the service, and he set up an occupational therapy unit with a difference. Basket weaving was not on his agenda; he wanted real and meaningful work for his patients and sought support from the aircraft industry. In association with aircraft instrument manufacturers Reid and Sigrist, a small satellite factory was set up in the hospital grounds managed by five of the company's staff to train the patients and check their work. In delivering the McIndoe Memorial Lecture in 1976, Russell Davis, the anaesthetist who worked with the surgeon for many years, spoke of the success of this initiative.

'... the patients were put to work making turn and bank indicators and other instruments. The patients were paid a small hourly rate for their work. After one year's operation two startling facts emerged: the production per man-hour was greater than that of the parent factory, while the rejection rate of tested instruments was less.'[76]

It was an extraordinary result from this first ever attempt to establish an industrial workshop within a hospital, a practice that is not uncommon today.

'Those poor boys,' Molly Tyler says, 'they worked so hard, they were determined to get it right but it was such a struggle with their poor fingers, and there was quite a bit of cursing went on, but they kept at it. I loved them and admired them so much.'

Molly, an occupational therapist, was in her early twenties and living in East Grinstead when, in 1943, she was offered the job as a supervisor in the workshop. 'I had to go away for two weeks to New Malden for training,' she tells me, 'and I had a baby boy and I left him with my mother while I was away. When I got back from the training on a Friday it was late in the afternoon, and raining. I was walking up from the station when I realised something was wrong and when I got to London Road I saw what had happened.'

Just after five o'clock that afternoon, a German bomber had dropped two 500-kilogram and eight 50-kilogram high explosive bombs across East Grinstead. One of each fell on the back of the stage of the Whitehall Cinema where the afternoon screening was coming to a close. The bombs fell without warning, and people streamed out of the cinema into the rain just as the aircraft flew back with the machine-guns turned on the panic-stricken survivors. Several people were killed outright, others were still trapped in the cinema, and the surrounding buildings were in flames.

'I was so worried,' Molly says. 'My mother had told me she was going to go to the pictures that afternoon and I knew she'd take the baby with her. And then I saw her crossing the road with him. She'd been uncomfortable in the cinema, she'd had a premonition that something was going to happen, so she'd left early, before the picture finished.'

Molly was initially intimidated by having to supervise the Guinea Pigs' work. 'Some of them were really clever pilots and engineers and I didn't feel right telling them what to do. I felt stupid trying to teach things to them but they were all for it. They were very cheeky too. They all had a sense of humour, and the sexy jokes and gestures they made with the pistons ... well you wouldn't want to know. They were wonderful boys. I was a bit of a favourite with them and they liked to flirt. I used to go dancing with them. Bill Foxley was a lovely dancer, and he took me to the other cinema, the Radio Centre, and I had to get out his money and put it on his hand so he could pay. They were such lovely boys.'

Public response to their appearance was the greatest challenge for Guinea Pigs once they left the hospital and the safe and friendly environment of East Grinstead.

Sandy Saunders was twenty-two and a lieutenant in the army when he was transferred to the Army Air Corps in 1945. 'That town did so much for us,' Sandy tells me. 'Being treated as we were by local people gave us hope. Of course when you went somewhere else it was very different, but at least you could believe that it was possible that people would one day see through the way you looked to the person beneath.'

During his elementary flying training as a glider pilot, he was caught in crosswinds as he attempted to land. After three attempts the plane crashed and burst into flames. Sandy escaped from the wreckage with his clothes on fire, and sustained forty per cent burns to his face, legs and hands. He was taken to the Queen Elizabeth Hospital in Birmingham, but his navigator was killed in the crash.

'That was a terrible time. I was trying to come to terms not just with my injuries but also with my failure which I felt had led to the death of the navigator. I was seriously depressed and suffering with flashbacks. I was suicidal. My face was horrible, I felt useless and I could see no life, no future. I couldn't believe that any woman would be able to look at my face and love me. Twice I went up onto the roof of the hospital with the intention of killing myself, and on both occasions it was a nurse who talked me down.'

Sandy underwent nine operations in Birmingham and when he was discharged he was appointed second-in-command of a prisoner-of-war camp near Derby. It was there that he learned what was happening at East Grinstead.

'I was having a lot of trouble closing my eyes, as the skin grafts on the lids had shrunk, and the medical officer at the camp told me what Archie McIndoe was doing at East Grinstead. So I picked up the phone and called the hospital and asked to speak to him, and he agreed to see what he could do.'

In a series of fourteen operations, McIndoe replaced Sandy's eyelids, did a nose graft and made a number of adjustments to the reparations that had previously been carried out on his face.

'That's what inspired me to train as a doctor, because at East Grinstead I saw the way medicine can turn your life around. I used to watch Archie performing operations to learn what I could from him. But it wasn't only surgery that saved me, but the town. Having a near-death experience gives you the inspiration to make the most of life and be more understanding of other people's problems.'

Sandy Saunders was in his eighties when we met, and still in general practice close to Melton Mowbray.

The challenge of acceptance was ongoing. Even after the war and into the 1950s ignorance about facial disfigurement was still widespread and people with facial injuries had to tolerate the shock, disgust and fear of others who caught sight of them. But, like Jack Toper in his battle to be allowed out of the offices and into the store with Marks & Spencer, most managed to rise above it and many were supported by the intervention and advocacy of McIndoe and the Guinea Pig Club.

McIndoe's concern for his patients was always whether, once having repaired their bodies, he and the Guinea Pig Club could also help to restore something of their shattered lives. Part of Edward Blacksell's role was to prepare the men for the outside world and build bridges with potential employers. In this respect it was Bill Foxley who presented the greatest challenge; he had lost his hands, had very limited sight, and an expressionless face. McIndoe and Blacksell felt he might be the one person who was unemployable. The work that went into restoring his body and face had been long and hard for Bill and for McIndoe's team, and it was Bill's faith in what they had done, and in his own physical fitness, along with his irrepressible spirit, that completed the task of rebuilding his life.

He worked on his fitness and developed a reputation as a runner, and when he was finally discharged he and his wife, Catherine, opened an ironmonger's shop in Devonshire. But Bill discovered that he was not an ideal shopkeeper and he struggled to handle nails, nuts and bolts. Eventually the club assisted the Foxleys out of the shop and they moved to Crawley, not far from East Grinstead. Bill spent most of his working life commuting to London where he worked with the Central Electricity Generating Board. Until his death in 2010 he, like many other members of the Guinea Pig club, remained committed to doing what he could for burned servicemen, especially those wounded in the Falklands War. There are many extraordinary tales of courage and determination on the part of English, Canadian and European Guinea Pigs who returned to active service, and built new lives after the war. But some fared less well, and one of those was Richard Hillary.

Following his treatment at East Grinstead, Hillary was determined to return to flying and had several bruising encounters with the medical board in order to be pronounced fit. In 1941 he came up with a plan to visit the USA, touring industrial sites, talking to war workers about the war effort, and also visiting community groups. He put his plan to the Ministry of Information where Duff Cooper and Sir Walter Monckton could see the potential of the idea but also foresaw problems. In the end it was the approval of the Air Ministry that was needed and eventually Hillary's enthusiasm and determination won through. McIndoe was cautious but backed him all the same, and arrangements were made for the trip.

Richard Hillary arrived in New York to be met by a small but enthusiastic media contingent at the Plaza Hotel. But in

Washington things looked rather different. Senior officials at the British Embassy were shocked by the sight of his face and believed that public appearances could only be counterproductive. They feared that the mothers of America 'would take one look at him and express their concern, saying: "We don't want our boys to die for Britain".'[77] Hillary was told he could not be allowed to tour, but officials agreed to have his planned speeches distributed as pamphlets, and he was allowed to record radio broadcasts during his stay.

Hillary appealed to Lord Halifax, then British Ambassador to the US, who in turn approached President Roosevelt urging him to support the tour, but was faced with a veto from the White House. Americans were not accustomed to seeing the wartime disfigurements that were becoming increasingly common in Britain, and it was felt that Richard Hillary's appearance would not be a useful or effective propaganda exercise.[78] Hillary was devastated and returned to London, his self-esteem, spirit and pride in tatters. Eventually he recommenced his efforts to return to flying despite the fact that his colleagues noted he could barely hold a knife and fork. His persistence was rewarded and he was declared fit for service but was unable to fly solo and retrained with the Operational Training Unit at Charterhall.

McIndoe, who had been away for a desperately needed break, was horrified when he heard the news. Not only was he anxious about Hillary's physical state and problems with his eyes that he felt could not stand the strain of night flying, but he was deeply concerned about his state of mind, believing him to be suffering from depression. McIndoe urged the RAF to ground Hillary until he had undergone further treatment. But no action was taken and by July 1942 he was back in the air flying light aircraft, and was cleared for operational flying by the medical board in November that year. But there were immediate problems: handling the heavy aircraft was almost beyond the capability of his badly damaged hands, and weather conditions exacerbated the difficulty of keeping control. He also struggled with operating some cockpit equipment. Despite being counselled to give up flying, at least until he made more progress towards full recovery, he persisted. In the early hours of the morning of 8th January 1943, shortly after take-off for a training flight in a Blenheim, Hillary was orbiting the airfield in low cloud cover accompanied by his radio operator Sergeant Wilfred Fison. The ground controller told him to circle a flashing beacon. David Ross writes that the controller asked, 'Are you happy?' and that Hillary replied, 'Moderately. I am continuing to orbit.' He was waiting 'for a decision to be made regarding a partner for the exercise ... When he was spoken to again a few minutes later there was no reply.' There was a high-pitched whine followed by a terrible crash.'[79]

Both Hillary and Fison were killed and their deaths were followed by recriminations over whether or not Hillary should have been allowed back into the air. But his bullish determination had been convincing, and officers had believed in him and admired his persistence and courage. Had Hillary been the sort of person who could have fully integrated himself into the brotherhood of the Guinea Pig Club, perhaps it is possible that he might have been persuaded to settle for living out the war on the ground. But flying was his passion, it was part of who he was and how he saw himself, and brotherhood did not transcend his need to remain a flyer. He had spoken and written of the solitary nature of the flyer and how those who volunteered for the war in the air needed a confident indifference to life and death. He never grew to accept the limitations of his wartime injuries, and his facial wounds seem to have done nothing to discourage the attentions of the many women attracted to him. Questions about a death wish have always been in the slipstream of his death, but his story lives on in *The Last Enemy* as a significant and poignant contribution to the literature of the Second World War.

*

Archibald McIndoe was enduring a gruelling war during which he worked very long days in the operating theatre, visited other RAF hospitals to advise on treatment, and fought long and robust battles with bureaucracy on behalf of his patients. He had created a therapeutic community in a small country town, and developed the instruments and procedures of plastic surgery that led to the sophisticated treatments being used in the twenty-first century. He took few breaks, fewer than he needed, and spent too little time attending to his own life and particularly to his family. And in 1943 he also faced problems with his hands that threatened his ability to operate, and his postwar career as a surgeon.

The problem began with stiffness in the ring finger of his left hand and a feeling of deadness in the right. For a while he continued operating and practised exercising his hands by squeezing a ball, just as many of his patients were doing to restore the movement and grip in hands stiffened by burns and trauma. It didn't take McIndoe long to diagnose Dupuytren's contracture—a condition in which the fingers slowly contract and curl into the palm. It is mainly found in men and usually men over the age of forty. Actors Bill Nighy and David MacCallum, US president Robert Reagan, prime minister Margaret Thatcher, playwright Samuel Beckett, and cricketers David Gower and Graham Gooch all suffered with this condition. It can begin rapidly and then slow down or, conversely, start slowly and rapidly speed up. McIndoe knew he must act swiftly before any finger contracted to a point at which it would be frozen for life. For a man who had spent his war in the effort to restore function in his patients, this was first-hand experience of the fear of being rendered useless in his chosen field.

The surgical procedure for Dupuytren's contracture was then, and still is, complex and risky, requiring an incision in the palm of the hand and extreme surgical skill in identifying the digital nerve for each finger so that the tissue causing the contraction can be cut away. Mosley comments that in this operation there is 'danger of a kind which only a pianist, an artist or a surgeon can understand.'[80] McIndoe entrusted his hand to his friend and partner, the surgeon Rainsford Mowlem, and was recovering in hospital in London two days after the operation when he got news of the bombing of the Whitehall Cinema in East Grinstead. Casualties were being admitted to the hospital, which was also faced with accommodating the bodies of those who had been killed. McIndoe was supposed to rest and particularly to take great care of his hand, but his concern over what might be happening at the hospital made rest impossible. Late that night he discharged himself from hospital, put his bandaged hand in a sling and drove home to East Grinstead, arriving in the early hours of the morning to supervise the management of the patients. His inability to do more than that frustrated him, and it gave him a horrifying insight into a possible future in which he might no longer be able to operate.

Stress and anxiety took their grip on him; he became irritable and depressed and although his hand continued to heal well, the darkness did not lift. A few months later he developed stomach pains, which eventually led to his belief that he had liver cancer. But as discussed earlier the scare proved to be due to a problem appendix. Once that was successfully removed the pain did not abate and the problem of the forgotten surgical swab was discovered and he underwent surgery again. It was a period of extreme pain and distress. McIndoe was unused to being vulnerable and unable to take control, and the pressure of this, along with the physical effects, took its toll.

As the war drew to its close the pressure lifted a little but McIndoe continued to work on every front: in the theatre, in teaching young surgeons, and in taking on various authorities on behalf of his 'boys'. He and Edward Blacksell fought battles for improvements in war and disability pensions and, always a devoted Tory, he believed the new socialist Labour government would level off living conditions in Britain with deleterious effects. Most of all he feared the introduction of the proposed National Health Service, believing it would lower standards of health care. He was determined to fight to save the Queen Victoria Hospital from State control and attempted to take on health minister Aneurin Bevan head to head. There were many more battles to come.

His involvement with and advocacy for his Guinea Pigs

continued, as did his enjoyment of their company over a sing-song around the piano, and pint or two in The Guinea Pig, a local pub close to the hospital which had been named for the men. Eventually, in 1947, he took a break to visit a friend, Robin Johnston, in Tanganyika and fell in love with Africa. Together with Johnston he bought a farm, which the latter ran for many years. McIndoe returned many times, combining work on the farm with some medical and surgical work in the local community. Time moved on and his marriage to Connie Belcham, his knighthood, and the widespread recognition and respect he commanded, ensured that the surgeon moved in powerful circles and high society. But he still kept working at East Grinstead and in London, ensuring that the ongoing operations needed by his Guinea Pigs were maintained, as well as operating on celebrities including Kay Kendall and Ava Gardner.

In 1960 the McIndoes took a trip to Spain, ostensibly for a holiday, but in fact to enable Archie to undergo cataract surgery in privacy. His eyes had been bothering him but he wanted to avoid creating doubt and uncertainty among current and future patients. The operation went well, but on the flight home he suffered a serious heart attack. It was another sign that his body was failing and in the months that followed he felt that decline in many ways.

On the 11th April, after an evening spent eating and drinking with friends at White's club in London, Archibald McIndoe was driven home in the small hours. Later that morning, a maid who went to wake him with a cup of tea discovered that he had died in his sleep. The hospital staff, his patients and former patients reeled in shock at their loss.

'That was a terrible time,' Bob Marchant recalls. 'It was like a great big black cloud came over all of us. But we had to carry on because there were patients needing operations. It took a big effort and the place just wasn't the same, but somehow we kept going.'

The funeral of Sir Archibald McIndoe was held at St Clement Dane's and the church was packed with fellow surgeons and those he had trained, with friends, admirers and grateful former patients. Prominent among the guests were his beloved Guinea Pigs. His legacy has become a legend and his pioneering work in plastic surgery built the foundations for the future. He had hoped that within his lifetime he would be able to develop a research unit that would uncover some of the mysteries of human skin and tissue, and the possibilities of the surgical replacement of limbs and organs. Sadly he did not live to see it happen, but the Blond McIndoe Research Foundation was built, and it remains as a national and international tribute to his extraordinary skill, talent, innovativeness and sheer bloody-minded determination to push out the boundaries of surgery and take on the bureaucracies that stood in the way of progress. Now, decades later, the men with McIndoe's faces are proof not only of his pioneering surgery but his innovative work in establishing a therapeutic community in a small town, and a patient support group that is still working for its members.

'We are the Trustees of each other,' Archibald McIndoe wrote in the *Guinea Pig* magazine in 1944. 'We do well to remember that the privilege of dying for one's country is not equal to the privilege of living for it.'[81]

20. THE TOWN THAT DIDN'T STARE

October 2007

My time here is running out and I am torn between wanting to see my family and friends in Australia and wanting to hold on to what I have rediscovered here. One of the wettest, coldest summers on record has given way to the start of a glorious autumn. The trees are turning to red and gold and bright, chilly mornings give way to clear skies and sunshine. The days are beautiful, but so short. How early the darkness falls now the clocks have changed. How long the evenings seem. However did I live through winters when it is almost dark by four o'clock? I spend time checking back through my typewritten and handwritten notes, and the stack of documents I've photocopied in various libraries, and I find something I had temporarily forgotten. Titled 'The Town That Doesn't Stare' it is an article from the *Reader's Digest* of November 1943, four months after the bombing of the Whitehall cinema when 108 people were killed and 235 were injured; the largest single wartime loss of life in Sussex. The town had already been attracting national attention thanks to Archibald McIndoe's groundbreaking work at the hospital.

'East Grinstead,' the article begins, 'is a town with a broken heart and a heartbreaking job.'

And it goes on to describe the presence of the Guinea Pigs who come into the town each day 'with their shapeless, raw, red faces'.

'They walk down the street, trying not to see themselves in shop windows, their curled and sometimes fingerless hands in their pockets. Their faces are not of this world during the long period of skin grafting. Often the nose or both the ears are gone. Their eyes are tiny, bleak glistening marbles, and the look in them is not one to write about. The first time you see one of these boys the blood goes out of your face and your stomach rocks. You curse yourself but you can't help it.'

The writer goes on to describe how local people stop and talk to the men in the street, take them into their homes; how girls invite them to dances, and even the children don't stare. 'So, in East Grinstead the most ghastly burned boy is the most welcome. His face is the job of the hospital, but his will to live is a job that is in the hands of the townsfolk.'[82]

In the last couple of months my rose-tinted nostalgia for the England of my childhood has been dented by acknowledgement of the harsher reality of the times. Studying postwar photographs of London I have been reminded of the hardship and devastation of people who were robbed of everything and whose trauma and loss continued long after the peace. I have remembered visits in the early 50s to my paternal grandmother who lived in the East End. Her home was a neat and narrow terraced house in a surprisingly undamaged street, but getting there involved a walk through impoverished areas still awaiting repair and rebuilding: glimpses through windows into bleak half-furnished rooms in houses occupied by several families all living in poverty, ragged children playing in the ruins of buildings, and searching for treasure on rubbish dumps. My postwar childhood in the Sussex countryside, in beautiful undamaged villages and a comfortable home, is a world away from what others were surviving in London and the towns and cities of the industrial north. Even close to home, the poverty line existence of Evelyn's family, the deprivation and the cruelty of her young life, should always have been a reminder to me of my own incredible good fortune as a streak of gold in a harsh and gloomy cultural landscape.

But while these tough reminders of reality have affected me deeply, and helped me to understand how I have created my own memorialisation, it does not diminish the significance of what happened in this pleasant country town. What happened here in East Grinstead, what it says about its people and its ethos, is also real, and it is precious. This was a community that worked together to save the lives and mend the broken hearts of young men, and saved its own wartime heart in the process. If that could happen here, then it could and did happen in other contexts in towns and villages around the country. My memories are of a way of life, a way of thinking and being which, while there were many things wrong with it, still enabled this to happen and to continue until the waves of change that swept across Western Europe in the 60s. Awareness and a realistic view is good, but I don't have to give up on what I still think of as 'my England'.

And so I indulge myself by setting off on a trip that is pure nostalgia; no one to meet or interview, no notes to take, or calls to make, no appointments to keep, just time to revisit the places of memory. I drive first through Ashdown Forest following the route that I travelled so often with my mother in a double-decker bus, to visit my grandparents in the village of Alciston near Eastbourne. Driving now along a wooded stretch, I remember clutching the thick metal handrail of the front seat on the top deck and looking out across a dense carpet of bluebells, where a big red fox sat, lazily scratching himself in a patch of sunlight as the bus lumbered past. The image is as clear as if it were yesterday and it brings tears to my eyes.

I was born in the East End of London in February 1944 – the period known as the 'Baby Blitz', when Greater London and South East England took a considerable beating. A few weeks later, my father decided that it would be safer if he moved Mum and me out of town. He rented a cottage in Alciston, about fifteen minutes walk from Grandma and Grandpa, and Mum and I stayed there while Dad commuted back and forth on weekends when he didn't have duties in his volunteer work as a special constable. In Alciston I park the car near that cottage. I have no conscious memory of the year or so that we lived here, but the place is familiar from postwar childhood visits and Mum's stories of our time here.

Leaving the car, I set out in the clear sunlight of an autumn afternoon to walk back along the road, past the pub, to the lane where my grandparents lived, the route Mum walked most days, with me in the pram or pushchair. In June that year, as the Baby Blitz came to an end, this place was right in the flight path of the Doodlebugs—V1 and V2 bombers fired from launch sites along the French and Dutch coasts for the terror bombing of London.

'I would hear them coming,' Mum told me many times. 'That buzzing noise they made, and I'd either run the last bit of the way, or I'd tip the pushchair into the ditch with you in it and then climb in on top of you. It happened so often that I could swear they waited for me to leave the cottage and get halfway down the lane and then in they'd come. You used to scream your head off at the sound of those bloody things. Terrible, menacing things they were, like some great monster creeping up on us. Something about them made me feel they had our names on them.'

More than one hundred V1s a day were fired at south-east England, a total of 9,521 between June and October, but we escaped. Today the banks of the same ditch are scattered with daises and fading cow parsley, as they would have been then. My grandparents' cottage is still here, its sentinel pine trees on either side of the front gate, and the view across the fields remains as it would have been then and as I have always known it.

Later I stroll along the seafront at Eastbourne alongside the colourful beds of flowers, and narrow three-storey terraced houses with flaking paint, offering bed and breakfast, or announcing 'no vacancies'. It's windy and the sun is dying as I make my way onto the pier, passing angry seagulls fighting over a dropped bag of chips. The sharp and salty scent of the sea and the crash of waves on the pebbled beach bring other, later, childhood memories: holidays on sand and pebbles with a bucket and spade; ice-cream cones, and a scratchy bathing costume ruched with shirring elastic; the smell of cockles and whelks sold from a tiny kiosk; the balm of calamine lotion on sunburn in the late afternoon.

The following day I drive from Hartfield, through East Grinstead and out on the main road towards Crawley and Gatwick Airport and stop outside the house where I lived from the age of nine until I married in 1965. It is a renovated Tudor cottage, with white-painted wattle and daub walls, black timber beams and diamond-paned, leadlight windows. Centuries ago it was an overnight stopping place for smugglers making their way from the south coast to London to trade their whisky, lace, tobacco and silver. Alongside the house a narrow, muddy footpath cuts through for a quarter of a mile, between two parallel roads, separating the house from its own land. The owner from whom my parents bought the house in 1953 had lived here since the 30s and at one stage objected to the footpath and attempted to have it officially closed and removed from the ordnance survey maps. His efforts were met with the old Sussex tradition of Rough Music. Every night for a couple of weeks, local men gathered outside the house with dustbin lids, buckets, spades, and other metal tools or containers, and raised an almighty din of metal on metal, for several hours at a time. The local council turned down the application, and the path remains, muddier than ever and even more overgrown than it was in my childhood. I make my way through the tangled mass of brambles and overgrown bushes until I can see through to what was, in my time, a couple of acres of neatly planted fruit bushes, and beautifully trimmed lawns, dotted with massive rhododendron bushes. Here Evelyn and I batted tennis balls around, and collected seeds and leaves, steeping them in water to make imaginary wine or tea in old tin cans. Here we crawled into the sheltered darkness of the rhododendrons to whisper our secrets and make our plans. Beyond the impassable net of prickles and broken branches is the huge copper beech tree. An indistinguishable mass of high brambles hides the place on the lawn where my father erected a marquee for my wedding reception.

Peering across the tangled remains of the garden, I am filled with rage at the neglect of what was once so meticulously maintained. But really my rage and sadness is at my own neglect for all that I left behind in my youthful push to move on to something new, something different, more exciting, more modern.

*

A few days later, still suspended somewhere between past and present, I shake out my one reasonably formal dress and prepare for the Guinea Pigs' dinner at the Felbridge Hotel, where I first met Jack Toper. The Felbridge was always popular with the men but it was The Whitehall restaurant and pub, part of the entertainment complex in the centre of the town, that was their favourite watering hole and which came to feel like their own social club. The manager, Bill Gardner, not only ensured they were well looked after, but became a friend to his regulars and kept a wary eye on their drinking habits, packing them off back to the hospital when he felt they'd had enough. The Guinea Pigs were always welcome at The Whitehall as they were in the other pubs in town, the shops and the cinema. The community's embrace of these injured young men was the result of McIndoe's determination to pave the way for their acceptance. In addition to his own efforts to involve locals in creating a safe place for the Guinea Pigs, he urged not only the hospital committee but his staff to talk to people in the town and encourage them to ignore the faces and greet the heroes.

Margaret Streatham remembers a friend who worked in a local café, telling her that the staff had discussed how to behave to the men and agreed to make a special effort to make them feel at home. Likewise, Edward Bishop records that Mabel Osbourne, a waitress at The Whitehall, spoke of a meeting of the staff there where they all agreed to '... look them full in the eyes and just see them, and treat them as if we don't see it. We'll look at them and not look away from them and speak to them. And that's what we did ... and we got so used to it that we never took any notice after that.'[83]

At the adjacent Rainbow Ballroom there was always a contingent of Guinea Pigs in various states of repair and reconstruction ready to dance and flirt with the local girls.

And for those Guinea Pigs who could get out and about there were invitations to private homes, for a drink or Sunday lunch, the chance to play music on a gramophone, a sing-song around the piano, or a game of cards. And just like Margaret Streatham and her mother, many local families doubled up to make room for wives, mothers and girlfriends who were visiting men destined for a long stay at the hospital.

Along with the convalescent accommodation provided in large homes like those of the Dewars and the Blonds, many other families opened their homes to men who were far from their own homes, inviting them to stay for a few weeks before moving back into the world beyond the safe haven of the town. A couple of weeks after my nostalgia trip, when I met local historian Michael Leppard in his office at the East Grinstead Museum, he spoke of that special relationship between the townspeople and their wartime heroes. 'Sir Archibald's therapeutic community worked for his patients and for the town,' he told me. 'By involving people in that way he gave them a focus, took their minds off their own anxiety, and gave them a chance to do something for the war effort; something that had instant and tangible effects, where they could see the value of doing their bit. It was remarkable the way the town adopted the men, and it's refused to let go of them ever since.'

On the morning of the reunion dinner I am sitting in the Costa Coffee café in London Road, not far across the street from the site of the old Whitehall, when two elderly men and their wives make their way to a nearby table with a tray of coffee. I watch them settle into their seats and one of the men unloads the tray and gets up to return the tray to counter.

'I can take that for you,' says a young woman, sixteen perhaps or seventeen, who is wiping the tables, and then she stops. 'You're one of those Guinea Pigs, aren't you?'

The man's face is turned away from me and I can't hear his reply, but I see the girl smile, and her voice is loud above the noise of the café.

'Nan was a little girl in the war and her mum used to help up at the hospital. Two of your friends used to go to her for their Sunday dinner.'

The Guinea Pig gestures to her to join them at the table and she is talking excitedly with the four of them when a young man in a Costa uniform stops by the table and asks her what she thinks she's doing.

'They're Guinea Pigs,' she says. 'You know, from the war.'

And again I can't hear but I can see the young man speak and smile, and lean across the table to shake one good hand and one stump, before he too pulls up a chair and joins them. The legend lives on, passed from one generation of locals to the next.

*

The room is packed with people, mainly elderly people; there are sequins and dinner jackets, silk dresses and patent shoes, hearing aids and walking sticks, reconstructed faces and hands, and a joyful sense of excitement as people greet old friends and others sip their drinks and reminisce. Edging their way through the crowd are RAF cadets in uniform, selling raffle tickets, and refreshing glasses that have run dry. I can see Emily Mayhew introducing a man with a vaguely familiar face to a small group on the other side of the room, and realise it is A. A. Gill, journalist, reviewer, commentator, and columnist for many prestigious publications including *The Tatler*, *Vanity Fair* and *The Sunday Times.* Adrian Anthony Gill has an acid pen and a total lack of reverence for groups and institutions that many hold dear. His writing is sharp, clever and brutal and he has an unparalleled record of complaints against him to the Press Council, particularly on issues of racism. I wonder why Gill has come, and hope that he will manage to cover this event with at least a modicum of restraint.

Bob Marchant kindly organised an invitation for me and it's a privilege to be here, but I feel exactly what I am, an outsider. It's not that I am ostracised; on the contrary I am welcomed into conversations with strangers and those I've already met. It is simply that the atmosphere is charged with intimacy and memory, with the recurring pleasures and pain of shared experience, and the awareness that this will be the last time they will all be together. The fallen from the distant and recent past are present in every conversation, as people cling to this final reunion. Dinner is served and the speeches are brief, entertaining and gracious; tonight is for the Guinea Pigs, their wives and other family members, some local dignitaries and other invited guests. Tomorrow, as always, there will be the real reunion; a dinner for the men alone with doors closed to all others with the exception of the club's Patron, HRH Prince Philip, Duke of Edinburgh.

The following morning, St Swithun's Church is packed with visiting Guinea Pigs, their nearest and dearest, East Grinstead residents and former residents, and current and former hospital staff, for the annual memorial service. This connection of the town to its long-term war heroes, its surgeon and its hospital continues more than sixty years after the end of the war and speaks volumes about the feelings and the values of the time, and the desire to carry that into the future.

As we file out of the church I catch snippets of conversation: 'the last time', 'won't be doing this again', 'may not see you again'. There are smiles and tears, silent emotional hugs, and hands mottled with age clasp each other and hesitate to let go. And yet it seems impossible to imagine these men not returning here, not gathering to share the old jokes and memories, or mourn the loss of old comrades. Something will surely be saved, and some things will go on forever.

21. FAREWELLS

On the morning of Saturday 24th November, I sit on the bed in the studio while a bitter wind rattles every door and window, and rain lashes the roof. I'm glued to my laptop and my spirits are rising as I watch the ABC's live feed of the final hours of voting in the Australian general election. My mobile beeps frequently as family and friends back home text me with messages about the prospect of a new government. And when I switch off in order to drive to Newmarket for a farewell dinner with my uncle and cousins, I'm positively lighthearted.

My cousins Ian and Chris have arranged to meet me at an easily located meeting point, and I follow them back to Chris's house. Ian and Chris's father, Laurie, is my father's younger brother, and later with my cousins' wives, Jean and Christine, we collect Laurie from his apartment and set out for dinner. Uncle Laurie, just turned ninety, is as smart as ever: dark blazer, regimental tie, thick silver hair slicked back, moustache neatly trimmed.

'My favourite niece!' he says.

'Your only niece.'

'Same thing,' he says. 'You'd always be my favourite even if there were others.'

He is certainly my favourite and only uncle, although he and Dad did have a younger brother whom my father virtually cut out of his life years before I was born, for reasons that have never been explained to me. My father, Len, and Laurie have always been similar in appearance, except that Dad had lost his hair as a young man. They are less similar though in nature. 'Len was the brains of the family,' Laurie told me once, 'I'm the brawn.' He certainly had some brawn as a builder in their father's family business, and later in the army, but he was never short on brains. He and his late wife Jean ran pubs for much of their lives; both of them cheerful, endlessly good-natured people and great hosts.

My dad was also good-natured and generous, but he lacked Laurie's outgoing personality. He was more often serious, had a strong sense of duty and self-discipline, and a need for control and order. Despite the fact that he was also very strong-minded and often outspoken, I have come to believe that his need for control and his almost unquestioning belief in and commitment to authoritative institutions had its roots in some sort of fear.

'I remember you being born,' Laurie tells me over dinner. 'February nineteen forty-four, we were in the desert and I got a telegram from Len. Dear old Len, I still miss him.' He talks about his war, his evacuation from Dunkirk, and then the desert war. 'Poor Len, of course, he never really got over not being able to enlist. He took that very badly.'

This surprises me as I never heard Dad express any sort of emotion about not having been in the armed services. I was told he was in a reserved occupation with the Ministry of Supply, so was compelled to remain in it. He was responsible for the distribution of supplies of food and equipment to industrial canteens. Wanting to serve in another way he also signed up as a volunteer special constable with the police. I say this to Laurie and he gives me a long, slightly bewildered look.

'Is that not right?' I ask.

He shifts, uncomfortably in his seat. 'Well yes, and ... no. But I suppose there's no harm you knowing now. It was an important job but it wasn't a reserved occupation. That's not why he couldn't enlist; the thing was ...' and he pauses.

It began, he tells me, when in his late teens Len became a supporter of Oswald Mosley. Mosley who had been a Conservative Member of Parliament, and then an Independent, had spent a few years outside Parliament, and then joined the Labour Party, winning the seat of Smethwick in 1926. By 1929 Mosley had joined the Fabian Society and when Labour won the election that year he was given the responsibility for solving the unemployment problem.

'Soon after that Len got involved,' Laurie says, 'he would've been eighteen, maybe nineteen. Mosley was a brilliant speaker; he won people over with his speeches. I suppose you'd call him charismatic.'

Mosley had developed what was known as the 'Mosley Memorandum', a plan that called for the nationalisation of some industries, high tariffs to protect others, and a massive public works program to deal with the unemployment problem.

'Len was very taken with that. He was going to meetings and handing out leaflets.' Laurie says. 'He thought Mosley had all the answers.'

But Mosley soon became dissatisfied with Labour and eventually resigned his ministerial position. In 1931 he lost his seat in the general election and as the leader of the New Party which he had formed, he went on a study tour of some of the new movements in Europe. It was after meeting Mussolini in Italy that he returned home with the belief that fascism was the answer to Britain's problems.

'It took Len a while to work out what was happening,' Laurie says. 'Anyway, by the time Mosley started his Black Shirts and the British Union of Fascists, he was out of it and a bit embarrassed about it all. But when he went to sign up, the army wouldn't have him. Security risk you see. It broke his heart not being able to serve his country. He was ... well he was very patriotic and he had a big thing about doing your duty. Dreadful business really; he'd only been a young lad when he got involved and he was out of it before he was twenty-one. When the army wouldn't have him, that's why he signed up as volunteer special constable.'

Even then, Laurie tells me, Dad didn't give up. During the Battle of Britain he tried again and once more, early in 1943, but he was knocked back each time. 'He didn't ever get over that. He never said it but I think after that, he felt like a suspect. It was the shame you see. That'd be why he never told you.'

We sit there facing each other, both of us with tears in our eyes.

'I hope you don't think less of him. Maybe I shouldn't have told you. He was all for King and Country, and duty ... I do believe it broke his heart.'

Much later that night, in the spare bedroom in Chris and Christine's house, I write down everything I can remember about my conversation with my uncle, and mull over what I have learned and what I think I now understand. I have speculated endlessly on the possible reasons why this rather straitlaced, law-abiding man, who tried so hard to do everything right, seemed to fear falling foul of authority. I now have another piece of the jigsaw.

Laurie explained that while Dad was grappling with the shame of his own situation, their brother Don, who had always been their mother's favourite, tried everything possible to avoid conscription on religious grounds. Their mother, a devout member of the local Baptist Chapel, did all she could to support him despite the fact that he had never set foot in the chapel since the age of thirteen, and had often taunted her with his own lack of belief. Len, Laurie and their father were disgusted at this and there were violent family rows and a split that never healed. Eventually Don's efforts failed and he gave up and enlisted in the navy. Dad never forgave his youngest brother for trying to evade active service, nor their mother for supporting him. So now the decades of estrangement make sense, as does the tension and antagonism between my father and his mother.

In the packet of old family photographs that I had brought along to share with Ian and Chris, I find two taken on my parents' wedding day in September 1939, the month that war was declared. They are in the corner of a panelled room, in a registry office in East London. My mother in a suit with a straight skirt, has a broad brimmed hat atop her marcel waved hair. She is sitting on a square, fabric-covered seat by a small occasional table. Sitting, I suspect, because she was four inches taller than my father. Her long, slim dancer's legs are neatly crossed at the ankle, and there is just a slight trace of a smile on her face. On the other side of the table, my father is standing, leaning very slightly towards her, his hand on a pile of books. He is in the uniform of a special constable. His handsome face is rigid with no trace of a smile, and in another similar photograph, his uniform hat has been exchanged for a tin helmet. My father was always a dapper man; there are photographs of him from the same era in white tie and tails, dinner jacket with black tie, plus-fours and tweeds, a belted gabardine raincoat and trilby hat. I have always wondered why he had chosen to marry in the uniform of the specials. But now I understand. Most men who were in the armed services and married during the war, proudly wore their uniforms that day. Dad, I believe, was saving face for the future, by wearing the only uniform allowed him. The longer I look at the photographs the more I see him as Laurie described him—a man with a broken heart. It seems to explain so much and I am devastated that it is too late for me to tell him how much I loved him, and that knowing what I now know would not have made a jot of difference.

*

'So have you got what you wanted?' Evelyn asks me when I arrive at her home the following evening for another farewell. 'From the Guinea Pigs,' she says. 'Did you get what you wanted from all this?

'I think so. I'm not sure. I won't really know until I work out what it all means.'

She rolls her eyes. 'Writers. You never get a straight answer from a writer. There always has to be a story and everything has to have a meaning.'

'You have a lot of writers hanging out here looking for meaning, do you?' I ask. And she laughs and throws a tea towel at me.

'Well, do you at least know how you're going to write the book now?' she asks later.

I settle for saying, 'I think so, possibly.' While what I really feel like doing is admitting that I actually don't have a clue and am more confused and wobbly about the whole thing than when I started.

'So what about this *meaning* thing,' she continues. 'Can't

you just write what happened to them?'

I take a deep breath and start to talk about the personal context, about memories and how we seek meaning in them, how we all, writers or not, build our memories into stories that say something about ourselves and the times and places in which they exist. How we make sense of and store the past.

'About your dad,' she says. 'It's sad. I was a bit scared of him, but he and your mum never let me feel there was anything – any distance between my family and yours, d'you know what I mean? Class difference, money. They made me feel I mattered. I never felt I mattered at home.' And she tells me again what she told me the first time we met in Perth after four decades without contact. My email through Friends Reunited had come as a shock. Years earlier she had drawn down the blinds on a truly horrible, poverty-stricken, abusive childhood, and had to think seriously about whether she wanted to revisit it, but my message had reminded her that there were also moments of pure happiness. 'Us being friends was the only sunshine,' she says now. 'And then you trying to find me again after nearly forty years, and you being here now. It means I mattered to you then and I still do. Is that enough meaning?'

We go on to talk of old times, of our parents and our schooldays.

'The other thing I learned from this,' I say, 'is that I understand how I always had this obsession about being good – the anxiety about getting some small thing wrong and the world collapsing around me as a result.'

'Mmmm. Well you *were* always annoying in that way when we were kids, scared about getting into trouble. I was always in trouble whatever I did so I didn't think much about it. But you haven't always been *a good girl* as an adult have you?'

'Well not always good,' I say, 'but always guilty and anxious when I strayed from it. And always nervous about being found out and suffering terrible repercussions.'

'And were you – found out?'

'Not really,' I laugh. 'Mostly I've managed to evade detection.'

'Oh well,' Evelyn says as she starts to stack the dishwasher, 'perhaps you'll work it all out once you're away from here. The Guinea Pigs, the war, your dad, all this other stuff too. Work it out back home.'

'Maybe,' I say. 'I hope so. Right now it's like a big black hole.'

'And what if you don't?'

I shrug and brush crumbs off the worktop. 'I'll have to wait until I do.'

'But that might be ages.'

'Yep. It might.' I don't feel anything like as cool about it as I sound. What if I never work it out?

*

Two days later I take a cab to Gatwick Airport, my last glimpses of the winter-green Sussex countryside washed away in torrential rain that reduces traffic to a crawl. I have been awake for most of the previous night struggling with what feels like bereavement. The intensity of it seems out of proportion to the fact that I am simply leaving England to go home to Australia, that I could realistically return here at any time in the future and most certainly will. But it feels as though something is over; something more than just a long stay in a place I love. Something has gone and although I am not yet clear what it is, I do know it's not something I'll get back.

Thirty-odd hours later I am in another taxi, still short of sleep, catapulted into the harsh brilliance of a West Australian summer. It's culture shock of a kind I remember when I first moved here from England, that uneasy feeling that so much is the same, and then the slow insidious reminders that these are, in fact, two profoundly different places in many obvious and many more subtle ways. For the first few days I struggle to recover, not simply from the jet lag but from the person I have been for the last six months. I feel around for the person I am here, slip back into her being, move from asking the questions to having to answer them: what was it like—how did it go—did they talk to you—did you find any nurses—how did it feel to be in England all that time—did you find that man from when you fell down the stairs—have you written any of it yet? Are you actually okay, because you seem a bit weird? Weird—yes exactly—out of place, uprooted. Happy to be back but sad to have left, and sadder still at the loss of something I cannot name.

In the week before Christmas I receive a Christmas card from Simon and Susie and a copy of the 2nd December edition of *The Sunday Times Magazine*. It has a fine full-colour spread of images of Guinea Pigs and their stories and A. A. Gill's own experience at that final reunion dinner. 'Sex and seduction became a large part of the recuperation at East Grinstead,' Gill writes. 'Someone said, pointedly, that you could barely open a cupboard in the hospital without an airman covered in bandages and a nurse covered in very little tumbling out.'[84]

I imagine Joyce, Alice, Gladys and others reading this and wonder how it makes them feel to see themselves, their professionalism and their personal struggles so easily and superficially dismissed. I fold the magazine and put it into a file box with the other papers and wonder what I am going to do with what I have learned.

22. JOINING THE DOTS

Christmas comes and goes, and we slide into 2008. The packages of books, photocopied documents, photographs and other material that I posted to myself before I left England, arrive in the mail and I unpack them, sort them into categories, change the categories several times and finally pack them into file boxes, label them and stack all except one under my desk at home, keeping at the front those that relate to the nurses. Somehow, in the next couple of months I write an article about them for an academic journal; it is the first outcome required by the university as a result of my study project and must be submitted with my progress report. With this item out of the way I pack that last box of papers and the box joins the others under the desk.

'How's it going?' Evelyn asks, mid-year when we talk on the phone. 'You must be nearly finished by now.'

I'm thankful we are not on Skype and she can't see my flush of embarrassment. 'It's slow,' I lie. The truth is that I haven't even started. 'It's going to take quite a lot of time.'

'But you did so much here, interviews and research, and you were stuck at your laptop for days on end transcribing things. I thought you just had to write it now.'

And I try to explain that my struggle is *how* to write it, how to frame it. How the stories of the Guinea Pigs, the nurses, the town, and my own story all come together. I know that they do, but I still don't know why, nor why I had to do it or where that's taken me.

There is a somewhat disapproving silence at the end of the line, then Evelyn changes the subject and we move on to talk of other things. Long after that conversation I continue to think about the fact that although my irrational fear and my dreams of being crushed or smothered continue, the Guinea Pigs are no longer a part of them. Something has changed, even if I still don't know what that means.

From beneath the desk the boxes exude waves of guilt-inducing disapproval. Eventually I decide that all I need is a bit of discipline. So I put the boxes in the car and take them to the office, promising myself that I will devote a minimum of one day a week to work on the book. I will be rigorous with my timetable, will not leave the office until I have finished that day's work, and soon I will have established a habit. I'll get into the flow and increase the time to two days a week. Soon I won't be able to stop myself.

Six months later—a year after my return home—I still haven't opened the boxes. I still haven't written a sentence, let alone a chapter. The sense of failure increases the paralysis.

To anyone who writes, the myriad excuses and reasons we manufacture for not starting a piece of work will be very familiar. I've never had any patience with the concept of writer's block. For decades I was a freelance journalist and writer. If I didn't write I didn't get paid. Feeding one's children is a powerful incentive, and in any case I *am still writing*, most days, every day, for hours on end, including weekends—I'm just writing other things. And there are always other things to write. My friends have stopped asking about my progress, they have forgotten all about it. Colleagues remember it though. What about that book? How's it going? I develop a tortured artist expression. 'Just haven't had time to get to it yet,' I say shaking my head sadly. 'Pressure of other work.' They nod knowingly, and we talk about increased administrative demands, the constant introduction of new software systems, unreasonable demands for record keeping and students who can't get their act together. Who will not empathise with this? Well Evelyn doesn't, that's for sure.

'Bullshit,' she says, when I go back to England to visit my grandchildren. 'Make time.' But another year passes, along with one more and another trip during which I discover more sources in different archives, which also fail to do the trick.

Then, late one night, reading in bed, I come across a paragraph in a story by F. Scott Fitzgerald, that stops my breath, and I read it again, and again.

> He wanted to care, and he could not care. For he had gone away and he could never go back anymore. The gates were closed, the sun was down, and there was no beauty left but the gray beauty of steel that withstands all time. Even the grief he could have borne was left behind in the country of youth, of illusion, of the richness of life, where his winter dreams had flourished.[85]

I turn out the light and lie in the darkness. And at last I comprehend that this is all about the loss of innocence: the stories of the Guinea Pigs, the nurses, the town and the force of my own longing to recover the England of my childhood—each one is a story of lost innocence. Why has this taken me so long to understand?

*

A month later I have written three rather rough chapters, but at least I've started and when, some time later, I mention it to a publisher her enthusiasm edges me on. The boxes are opened, their contents stacked across my desk and table in my office. I can see some shape and order now. In November 2012 as I prepare to head back to England again for a short, pre-Christmas visit, I take a last look at the various piles of material, lock my office and leave.

The flight to England is, as always, deadly. I arrive feeling not just jet lagged but unwell, with an unrelenting headache and a cough. But England in winter can be beautiful; it is bright and clear with heavy frosts that clothe the streets and parks and last all day. I cough my way through the first week and am woken one night by a phone call from the properties office at the university.

'It's two in the morning here,' I groan.

'Sorry, didn't know you were overseas. Just wanted to

let you know that there was a big storm and the rain came through the roof and flooded your office.'

I struggle to sit up, a sick feeling in my stomach. 'Is there much damage?'

'Some books, and files and ...'

'The papers on my desk and table?'

'Pretty rough,' he says, 'soaked really, some were floating.'

I flop back onto the pillows with a sense of despair, and spend the rest of the night worrying what might or might not be lost. The next couple of weeks are cold and miserable. My five-year old, long-distance relationship—a relationship deeply rooted in shared cultural understandings of the postwar period, a very English sense of humour and left-wing politics—falls apart in the cruellest of circumstances. It had come to represent a sort of fusion between aspects of the past that I wanted to hold onto, and what I hoped for in the future. Frost turns to puddles, it begins to rain endlessly and I continue to cough and shiver my way through each miserable day with failing energy. It is a relief to head back home.

Thankfully, back in Perth, I discover that some colleagues have assiduously dried out much of my material, but some has been reduced to pulp and for several weeks it is difficult to work out what, exactly, has been washed away. Another Christmas comes and goes. Another year begins and I start work again, but I'm still coughing and feel completely exhausted. Some days putting one foot in front of the other is an effort; I walk the dog to the top of the road and wonder how I will make it home. I put it down to a combination of old age and a broken heart, and try to chivvy myself along. The only part of me that is working properly seems to be my brain. I tell myself I'll feel better when the weather gets cooler. But I don't. And for some reason I don't now understand I don't go to the doctor. In the middle of May I come to a grinding halt.

My nightmares are suddenly reality: I struggle to breathe, and throughout the long and scary night before I am taken to hospital my lungs creak and groan, like a decaying house, sweat coats my skin and I force myself to stay awake because if I close my eyes the walls will close in on me, the ceiling will collapse and I will disappear, smothered by piles of rubble.

Pneumonia. And there is something else that can't be identified. Tests are sent off and returned, a final test takes more than a week and when a result does arrive I learn that I have been harbouring the Legionella virus. There is evidence that I have been carrying this around for months and probably acquired it on the flight to London. With the diagnosis comes an antibiotic that will finally kill it off. But my brain has gone on strike now, for weeks I can barely think straight, let alone write, and am capable only of watching the most mindless reality television, and DVDs of the original black and white versions of the *The Forsyte Saga* and *Upstairs Downstairs*. It takes an unbelievably long time before I feel anything like normal.

Several months later, still recovering but back to writing, and struggling to find some resolution with this particular piece of work, I decide that with my seventieth birthday looming it is time I tried to get to the bottom of my fear. I have had enough of the nightmares, my unreasonable response to loud noises, the sudden pounding of my heart at news coverage of falling buildings, the terror of being smothered. Those horrible crashing suffocating dreams. Something deep within is always on fearful alert. My body is always tense, and I overreact to the smallest problems always imagining ridiculous outcomes—I will lose my family, my home, my freedom, in a flash it will all be gone. It makes no sense and I am sick of living like this.

'It's not really fear,' says the therapist, 'fear is logical, rational. You're swimming, you see a shark—that's fear and it's rational. But what you're telling me is not rational. It's phobia.'

And to my own surprise I start telling him about the Guinea Pigs, about how they were at the heart of the fear but are no longer a part of it. 'How can I get rid of the rest of it when I don't know where it comes from?' I ask.

'But it's obvious where it comes from,' he says. 'It's the war.'

'I was only a baby. I was under two when it ended. I have no conscious experience of the war. I don't remember it.'

'Not consciously, no,' he says. 'But your subconscious remembers. It remembers not just from when you were born but from when you were in the womb. Your mother – her fear when she was pregnant ... the air raids in London, the times she tipped you in the ditch ...'

And suddenly it is so blindingly obvious that I can't believe I have lived so long without working this out.

'Lots of people who have no conscious memory of the war are haunted by the sub-conscious knowledge of it. That's what we need to work on, it's really quite straightforward.' And I listen, eyes closed, as he talks about letting go.

It takes a surprisingly short time to rid myself of this fear that goes back further than I can remember. But go it does, taking the physical tension with it. I wonder what Evelyn would say to this. I imagine her drawing in her breath, shaking her head, and walking across her kitchen to fill the kettle. 'So I suppose there's a meaning to this too. Why does it always have to be so complicated with you?' And I laugh until the laughter turns to tears, because I can't tell her. Evelyn has gone. My last link to innocence, lost two years ago, to a slow-burning cancer that accelerated suddenly, and took her life in two terrible days. 'Well there's a thing,' I hear her saying, 'I never signed up for this.'

23. RESOLUTION

Perth, July 2014

On the wall above my desk is a framed copy of the testimonial that commemorates the fiftieth anniversary of the formation of the Guinea Pig Club in 1991, signed by Prince Philip and the then Chief Guinea Pig, Tom Gleave, and presented to me seven years ago by club secretary Jack Perry. On another wall there is a framed black and white photograph of East Grinstead High Street, dated 1947, the year my parents moved to the area from London. On the dresser in my bedroom is that strangely awkward photograph of my parents taken in London on their wedding day, and another of them taken here in Australia, when they were in their early eighties. They are smiling away from the camera, at a radio reporter who had stopped them in a shopping centre as he collected vox pops. My father has a broad but forced smile, my mother is more relaxed. When I look at them now I see a man with a broken heart, and a woman whose heart, I now suspect, was broken by trying to mend his. And on the fridge in the kitchen is a photograph of Evelyn and me, taken in 2004, the year we met again after decades without contact. It is fixed there by a magnet with a quote from French artist Louise Bourgeois, 'Art is a Guaranty of Sanity'. It seems a fitting thought as I try to find the words to pull these loose ends together. Although Evelyn, if she saw it, would have rolled her eyes and poured us a drink, as she had when I asked her if she had shared my childhood fear of the Guinea Pigs.

'No, I mean they did look awful, but I wasn't frightened of them. I never had dreams like you. But the war—it was everywhere; long after it was over, well into the fifties; the devastation, people talking about it. It was there like a big black cloud when we were kids. All of us, we were all affected by it.'

I had avoided responding because it wasn't how I remembered that time. In my blissful and privileged childhood we didn't mention The War; my home, the nearby town, the whispered conversations of women in the cafés, Miss Perkins tapping her stick on the floorboards at ballet practice, the nuns tucking up their habits and teaching us to make slides on the ice, was what I remembered. *'Pas devant ...'* my mother would murmur glancing anxiously at me if the subject was raised. She was, I am sure, protecting me; but what I now know makes me feel she was also protecting my father. The only darkness for me was those men at the bus stop, those faces, those shadows lurking in Blackwell Hollow, just the Guinea Pigs; and if only my dad or Sister Walbert would report them, have them sent away, then this blot on the landscape of childhood would be erased.

I never found the man from the staircase and now I wonder if he was real. I did fall down the stairs and awoke in the hospital, but was there a Guinea Pig, or was he perhaps a fragment of a dream that drove me from bed to the top of the stairs?

As I write this, my unease about the time it has taken has lifted. There *was* a story, many stories. There *was* purpose and meaning, and there were lessons to learn. It is seven years since I set off in search of Archibald McIndoe's Guinea Pigs and their nurses, but it has taken me almost seven decades to understand that the war was a part of me before I was even born.

REFERENCES

1. Memories

1. East Grinstead Observer, 27th July 1913, quoted in Osborne, Frances. *The Bolter*. Hachette, London, 2008, p. 43.

2. Beginnings

2. Mosley, Leonard. *Faces From the Fire: The Biography of Sir Archibald McIndoe*. Weidenfeld and Nicolson, London, 1962, p. 80.
3. ibid.
4. McLeave, Hugh. *McIndoe: Plastic Surgeon*. Frederick Muller, London, 1961, p. 71.
5. Dennison, E. J. *A Cottage Hospital Grows Up: The Story of the Queen Victoria Hospital, East Grinstead*. Anthony Blond, London, 1963, p. 82.
6. Mosley. op. cit., p. 46.
7. ibid., p. 51.
8. ibid., pp. 46.
9. ibid., pp. 47–48.
10. ibid., p. 71.
11. Mayhew, E. R. *The Reconstruction of Warriors: Archibald McIndoe, the Royal Air Force and the Guinea Pig Club*. Greenhill Books, London, 2004, p. 17.
12. ibid., p. 34.

3. Preparations for war

13. Milne, A. A. *The House at Pooh Corner*. Methuen & Co. Ltd, London, 1928, p. 122.
14. Mosley. op. cit., p. 82.

4. The burning question

15. Mayhew. op. cit., p. 58.
16. Fox, Angela. *Slightly Foxed*. Fontana, London, 1986, p. 82.
17. Mayhew. op. cit., p. 44.
18. ibid., p. 58.

7. The Guinea Pigs and their club

19. Francis, Martin. *The Flyer: British Culture and the Royal Air Force 1939–1945*. Oxford University Press, Oxford, 2011, p. 15.

20. ibid., pp. 18–21.
21. Churchill, Winston. Speech to the House of Commons, Westminster, 20/08/1940. churchill-society-london.org.uk/thefew.html.
22. Faulks, Sebastian. *The Fatal Englishman: Three Short Lives*. Hutchison, London, 1996, p. 129.
23. Bishop, Edward. *McIndoe's Army: The Story of the Guinea Pig Club and its Indomitable Members*. Grub Street, London, 2001, pp. 1–5.
24. Page, Geoffrey. *Shot Down in Flames: A World War II Fighter Pilot's Remarkable Tale of Survival*. Grub Street, London, 1999, pp. 112–113.
25. Mayhew. op. cit., p. 18.

8. On fear and silence

26. Bourke, Joanna. *Dismembering the Male: Men's Bodies, Britain and the Great War*. Picturing History Series, Reaktion Books, London, 1996, p. 175.
27. Fussell, Paul. *Understanding and Behavior in the Second World War*. Oxford University Press, Oxford, 1990, pp. 96–101.
28. Francis. op. cit., pp. 112–113.
29. Junger, Sebastian. *Why Veterans Miss War*: ted.com/talks/sebastian_junger_why_veterans_miss_war. January 2014.
30. ibid.
31. Francis. op. cit., p. 121.
32. Hillary, Richard. *The Last Enemy: The Memoir of a Spitfire Pilot*. Macmillan & Co. Ltd, London, 1943, pp. 52–53.
33. Dickey, James. 'The Firebombing', *The Selected Poems*. Wesleyan Publishing Inc., Indianapolis, 1998, p. 74.
34. Francis. op. cit., p. 113.

9. Life on Ward III

35. Mosley. op. cit., p. 80.
36. Chadd, Margaret. *Wartime Plastic Surgery Pt. 1*, BBC, WW2 People's War: bbc.co.uk/ww2peopleswar/stories/45a2423954.shtml. Accessed 12th September 2010.
37. Chadd, Margaret. *Wartime Plastic Surgery Pt. 2*, BBC, WW2 People's War: bbc.co.uk/ww2peopleswar/stories/89/a2424089.shtml. Accessed 12th September 2010.
38. Mosley. op. cit., p. 84.
39. ibid., p. 97.
40. Morris, M. Imperial War Museum Archives. (Misc 186) 80/38/1.
41. Mayhew. op. cit., p. 97.

12. Doing your bit for the war

42. Summerfield, Penny. *Reconstructing Women's Wartime Lives: Discourse and Subjectivity in Oral Histories of the Second World War*. Manchester University Press, Manchester, 1998, pp. 116–117.
43. Titmuss, Richard M. 'War & Social Policy', *Essays on the Welfare State*. George Allen and Unwin, London, 1958, p. 88.

44. Hinton, James. *Nine Wartime Lives: Mass Observation and the Making of the Modern Self.* Oxford University Press, Oxford, 2010, p. 12.
45. Summerfield, Penny and Crockett, N. '"You Weren't Taught That With the Welding": Lessons in Sexuality in the Second World War'. *Women's History Review,* 1, 3 (1992), pp. 435–454.
46. Hinton. op. cit., p. 7.

13. Pause for thought

47. McKibbin, Ross. *Classes and Culture: England 1918–1951.* Oxford University Press, Oxford, 1998, p. 307.

15. The Boss

48. Fitzgerald, Jim. Email, 15th September 2012.
49. Mosley. op. cit., pp. 166–167.
50. Mayhew. op. cit., p. 75.
51. Faulks. op. cit., p. 147.
52. Mosley. op. cit., p. 114.
53. Whittell, Giles. *Spitfire Women of World War II.* Harper Press, London, 2007, p. 3.
54. Chadd, Margaret. Wartime Plastic Surgery Pt. 3, BBC, WW2 People's War. bbc.co.uk/ww2peopleswar/stories/24/a2424124.shtml. Accessed 12th September 2010.
55. Mayhew. op. cit., p. 125.
56. Chadd, Margaret. Wartime Plastic Surgery Pt. 2, op. cit.
57. McLeave. op. cit., p. 119.
58. Page. op. cit., p. 114.
59. McLeave. op. cit., p. 144.
60. Mosley. op. cit., p. 192.
61. McLeave. op. cit., p. 181.
62. Mosley. op. cit., p. 222.
63. ibid., p. 226.

16. The outsider

64. Fussell. op. cit., pp. 109.

17. Face off

65. Carroll, Lewis. *Alice's Adventures in Wonderland and Through the Looking Glass.* Bantam Classics, London, 1984, p. 212.
66. Page. op. cit., pp. 86–88.
67. Simpson, William. *I Burned My Fingers.* Putnam, London, 1955, p. 31.
68. ibid., p. 33.

18. Emotional labour and war work

69. Rose, Sonya, O. *Which People's War? National Identity and Citizenship in Britain 1939–1945.* Oxford University Press, Oxford, 2003, p. 32.
70. Hochschild, Arlie Russell. *The Managed Heart: Commercialization of Human Feeling.* University of Californa Press, California, 1983, p. 5.
71. ibid., p. 38.
72. ibid., pp. 38–39.
73. Bolton, Sharon. 'Who Cares? Offering Emotion Work as a "Gift" in the Nursing Labour Process', *Journal of Advanced Nursing,* 32(3), pp. 580–586.
74. Lewis, Patricia. 'Suppression or Expression: An Exploration of Emotional Management in a Special Care Baby Unit', *Work, Employment & Society,* 19(3), pp. 565–581.
75. Hochschild. op. cit., p. 29.

19. Back to work

76. Davies, Russell. 'Relationships: Archibald McIndoe, his times, society, and hospital', McIndoe Lecture 1976, *Annals of the Royal College of Surgeons of England,* (1977) vol. 59(5), pp. 359–367. ncbi.nlm.nih.gov/pmc/articles/PMC2491805.
77. Ross, David. *Richard Hillary: The Definitive Biography of a Battle of Britain Fighter Pilot and Author of* The Last Enemy. Grub Street, London, 2003, p. 212.
78. ibid.
79. ibid., p. 330.
80. Mosley. op. cit., p. 162.
81. McIndoe, Archibald. 'The Maestro's Message', *The Guinea Pig,* 1944.

20. The town that didn't stare

82. 'The Town That Didn't Stare', *Reader's Digest.* November 1943.
83. Bishop. op. cit., p. 137.

21. Farewells

84. Gill, A. A. 'The Last of the Few', *Sunday Times Magazine,* 2nd December 2007, pp. 68–76.

22. Joining the dots

85. Fitzgerald, F. Scott. 'The Winter Dreams', *All the Sad Young Men.* Scribners, New York, 1926, p. 17.

ACKNOWLEDGEMENTS

Extracts from chapter 1 were previously published in 'The Man Who Wasn't There', eds. Glen Phillips and Julienne Van Loon. *Lines in the Sand: New Writing from Western Australia.* Fellowship of Australian Writers WA, 2008. Extracts from chapters 4 and 18 were previously published in Byrski, Liz (2012) 'Emotional Labour as War Work: Women Up Close and Personal with McIndoe's Guinea Pigs', *Women's History Review*, 21:3, pp. 341–361.

My thanks to the Faculty of Humanities at Curtin University for providing me with the time and funding for my initial research trip to England in 2007.

So many people have helped, supported and encouraged me in so many ways from the start of this project through to its completion and this book could not have been completed without them. My grateful thanks to those who assisted me in setting up the research trip:

Dr Emily Mayhew, of Imperial College, London, for providing essential information, encouragement and support prior to my trip, and for meetings in London on 8th August and 25th October 2007. For providing contacts, suggestions and contexts as well as answers to my many questions then, and in subsequent emails. I have relied heavily on her advice, and drawn on her book *The Reconstruction of Warriors: Archibald McIndoe, the Royal Air Force and the Guinea Pig Club.*

Simon Kerr, Tourism and Information Officer at East Grinstead Town Council, for assisting with contacts and the search for accommodation prior to my trip and for reintroducing me to East Grinstead and consistently providing me with information, updates, contacts both during my time there and since then. And to both Simon and Susie Kerr for their hospitality.

Sir Archibald McIndoe's daughter, the late Vanora Marland, gave generously of her time to correspond with me before I arrived in England and welcomed me to her home in Fulham on 7th August and 12th November 2007.

Since I began interviewing nurses, Guinea Pigs and their wives, friends, local residents and hospital staff for this book, many among them have, sadly, died. I thank them and those who remain for their generous participation in sharing their stories. I am especially grateful to the women who nursed the Guinea Pigs for speaking with me about their experiences at East Grinstead. For some this was the first time they had discussed their feelings and it was often difficult for them. I hope I have done justice to their stories. My thanks too, of course, to the Guinea Pigs, their wives and partners, who made me so welcome and told me their stories. It has been a privilege to meet both the nurses and the heroes whose words appear in these pages:

Bob Marchant who gave so generously of his time at several meetings and conversations at the Queen Victoria Hospital, and visits to the Guinea Pig Museum between 25th June and 30th November 2007, and for his patience with subsequent emails and questions.

Jack Toper, for meeting and talking with me at the Felbridge Hotel, East Grinstead, on 12th July 2007.

Bill Foxley, Tommy Brandon, George Holloway and Ray Brook with whom I shared drinks at The Hedgehog, Crawley, on 30th July 2007.

Dennis Neale, and Eunice Neale, for making me so welcome at their home in Witney on 17th July 2007.

Lady Moira Nelson, for her hospitality and a wonderfully enjoyable conversation at her home in Oxford on 16th July 2007.

Joyce* for meeting and talking with me at her home in Canterbury on 21st July 2007.

Jack and Mary Perry, for making me so welcome at their home in Abingdon on 18th July 2007, and for the gift of Guinea Pig related videos and my much valued copy of the testimonial commemorating the formation of the Guinea Pig Club.

Molly Tyler for sharing her memories of the Guinea Pigs with me at her home in East Grinstead on 19th July 2007.

Bridget Warner for kindly talking with me at her home in Croydon on 24th July 2007.

Gladys* who talked with me at her club in Kensington on 27th August 2007.

Nancy* who talked with me at her home in Dartford on 28th August 2007.

Arthur* who came to meet me at the Queen Victoria Hospital on 31st August 2007, where we shared warm memories and discussed his time in Ward III. And to his niece, Angela Greenslade, who brought us together.

Alice* who invited me to her home in Chorleywood and told me of her nursing experiences on 15th October 2007.

Alan and Ella Morgan for their warm welcome and generous hospitality at their home in Romiley, 29th October 2007.

Derek Martin for his contribution to my knowledge of the Guinea Pig Club and for telling me his story, during an interview at his home in Colnbrook, 21st August 2007.

Betty Parrish for a delightful conversation over coffee in Lingfield on 23rd October 2007.

Margaret Streatham, for a conversation in her home in Caterham, 6th September 2007.

Sandy Saunders, for our meeting and conversation at his surgery in Melton Mowbray, 31st October 2007.

Jane Lyons, for our conversation in the café at the British Museum, London on 9th October 2007.

Celia Hewett, who invited me to tea at her home in Paddington, London on 25th October 2007.

Michael Leppard for a meeting in his office in the East Grinstead Museum on 9th November 2007.

Malcolm and Barbara Valentin for being wonderful landlords during my stay in their studio in Hartfield.

And my thanks too to the other Guinea Pigs, nurses, local residents and dancing partners who spoke to me on the telephone or in emails but who are not named here.

Many academic colleagues and friends have encouraged and supported me in a variety of ways, and I am grateful for their advice and continuing interest: Dr Helen Merrick, Professor Colin Brown, Professor Tim Dolin, Dr Rachel Robertson, Dr Ron Blaber, Professor Jon Stratton and Professor Graham Murdock.

Working with Fremantle Press has been an enormous pleasure and I am grateful for all the work that has gone into getting this book into print. From the day I casually pitched the idea of this book to her over a cup of tea at the Perth Writers Festival, Georgia Richter believed it would happen and that it would work. Her enthusiastic encouragement, forensic editing and her insight into aspects of the story with which I struggled have contributed immeasurably to the finished product. Thank you so much Georgia. My thanks too to Clive Newman; and to Jane Fraser, Claire Miller and everyone else at Fremantle Press.

Finally, to my family, for their love, support, unwavering loyalty and encouragement in everything I try to do. I am so very fortunate to have you all.

Liz Byrski

For further information

The Guinea Pig Museum Collection is now housed in the East Grinstead Museum: eastgrinsteadmuseum.org.uk/guinea_pig_club.

Information on the Blond McIndoe Research Foundation can be found at: blondmcindoe.org.

First published 2015 by
FREMANTLE PRESS
25 Quarry Street, Fremantle 6160
(PO Box 158, North Fremantle 6159)
Western Australia
www.fremantlepress.com.au

Also available as an ebook.

Consultant editor Georgia Richter
Cover design Tracey Gibbs
Cover image adapted from a detail of 'Ward III at Christmas 1941', reproduced with kind permission of East Grinstead Museum
Printed by Everbest Printing Company, China

National Library of Australia
Cataloguing-in-Publication entry

Byrski, Liz, author.
In love and war: nursing heroes.

ISBN 9781925161458 (paperback)

World War, 1939–1945—Biography
World War, 1939–1945—Medical care
Nurses—Great Britain—Biography

940.547541

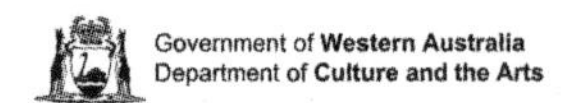

Fremantle Press is supported by the State Government through the Department of Culture and the Arts. Publication of this title was assisted by the Commonwealth Government through the Australia Council, its arts funding and advisory body.